SWEET POTATO LOVE

Also by Jackie Garvin

Biscuits: Sweet and Savory Southern Recipes for the All-American Kitchen

SWEET POTATO LOVE

60 RECIPES FOR EVERY SEASON

Jackie Garvin

Skyhorse Publishing

Skyhorse Publishing books may be purchased in bulk at special discounts for sales promotion, corporate gifts, fund-raising, or educational purposes. Special editions can also be created to specifications. For details, contact the Special Sales Department, Skyhorse Publishing, 307 West 36th Street, 11th Floor, New York, NY 10018 or info@skyhorsepublishing.com.

Visit our website at www.skyhorsepublishing.com.

10 9 8 7 6 5 4 3 2 1

Library of Congress Cataloging-in-Publication Data is available on file.

Cover design by Jane Sheppard
Cover photo credit: Jackie Garvin

Print ISBN: 978-1-5107-0966-9
Ebook ISBN: 978-1-5107-0972-0

Printed in China

Dedicated to Sam Garvin

Forty years of marriage,

Three children by birth,

Two children by marriage,

Three grandchildren,

Two bassett hounds,

Innumerable happy times

shared and doubled.

Heart-wrenching sad times

shared and halved.

One wonderful life

together—forever and

beyond.

Amen.

CONTENTS

Dedication
v
Sweet Potato Life
ix
Sweet Potatoes and Me
xviii

Chapter 1: Fall
1
Chapter 2: Winter
39
Chapter 3: Spring
75
Chapter 4: Summer
111

Resources
147
Acknowledgments
149
Bibliography
150
Index
151
Conversion Charts
163

Sweet Potato Life

Sweet potatoes have always been a part of Southern culture and foodways. They were one of the native American plants discovered by Christopher Columbus on his voyage to America. Evidence shows that sweet potatoes were included in the first Jamestown feast, a celebration that occurred a few years after the establishment of the colony in 1607. Sweet potatoes were not popular in Europe and not suited to the climate, so the English settlers were not familiar with them. The largest local tribe of Native Americans, the Powhatan Confederacy, taught the settlers how to cultivate sweet potatoes.

Just as the Jamestown, Virginia, settlers discovered soft winter wheat that eventually transformed biscuits from hard tack to the highly favored modern biscuit, which is soft and flaky, those settlers adopted the sweet potato introduced to them by Native Americans. The sweet potato has been a part of Southern culture ever since. Another similarity to biscuits is that for a long while, sweet potatoes' popularity in the United States was limited to the southern states but now enjoys nationwide rock star status.

Nutrition

The nutritional composition and low glycemic index of the sweet potato make it suitable for most any type of diet. Additionally, the versatility of the sweet potato makes it well-suited for all types of dishes: sweet and savory, appetizers, main courses, desserts, snacks, and breakfast. The Center for Science in the Public Interest (CSPI) ranked sweet potatoes as the number one vegetable in nutrition out of eighteen vegetables studied. Rich in antioxidants, anti-inflammatory nutrients, and blood-sugar regulating nutrients, sweet potatoes are power boosters and superfood heroes. They're a key source of beta-carotene and an average serving (3.5 ounces) may supply the recommended daily requirements of vitamin A. They're also an excellent source of vitamin C and potassium.

I Yam What I Yam

With a tip of the hat to Popeye, the Sailor Man, the sweet potato's classification might be surprising. The vegetable many called yams that makes an appearance on modern Thanksgiving tables in the United States isn't a yam at all. It's a sweet potato. The contents of the can of yams used to make candied yams doesn't contain yams either. These are sweet potatoes, too. Check the label. The contents are sweet potato, water, and usually some sugar.

People will argue that the fresh product in the grocery store is a yam if it's lighter in color than bright orange, but a yam is yam. A sweet potato is a sweet potato. They aren't even distant cousins.

A true yam is starchy, dry, and white fleshed with rough and scaly skin. The flesh isn't very sweet. A sweet potato has smooth skin and the sweet, moist flesh can range in color from white to orange to purple. It's unlikely that true yams are produced commercially in the United States. They're primarily grown in Africa, Asia, and the Caribbean, but there's a slew of sweet potato farmers in the United States, primarily located in North Carolina, Louisiana, Mississippi, and California. In addition, backyard sweet potato gardeners abound. Yams are of the genus *Diascorea.* Sweet potatoes are of the genus *Ipomoea* and are closely related to the morning glory. The blooms and leaves are similar.

Once I ordered yams in Barbados, West Indies, from a restaurant menu prior to my knowledge of the difference in true yams and sweet potatoes. At that time, I thought they were the same and expected sweet potatoes. I remember leaving the restaurant thinking they must have received a bad shipment of the worst sweet potatoes in the world. The vegetable on my plate was tasteless and dry, and not a sweet potato.

Roots versus Tubers

We eat the part of the sweet potato we call the root. This is where all its nutrients are stored. Since the sweet potato is a root, unlike the white potato that's a tuber, the sweet potato isn't able to produce "eyes." Instead, it puts off new growth known as slips.

Planting and Growing

Unlike white potatoes, which prefer a cooler environment, sweet potatoes are tropical plants that thrive in hot climates. They don't like rich soil and will perform the best in sandy soil.

Planting takes place after all danger of frost is over. Sweet potatoes are cultivated from a slip, which are seedlings cut from the mature sweet potato. The vines grow rapidly and produce a ground cover. Once the plants are established, they require little care outside of weekly watering. They grow for three to four months before reaching a suitable size to harvest.

Harvesting, Processing, and Curing

Jason Bell, sweet potato broker.

Sweet potatoes are ready for harvest in the fall. Stored in optimal conditions, they'll last about eight months. The new harvest comes in about the same time last year's harvest has been consumed or gone bad. The long shelf life keeps sweet potatoes available all year long.

When commercial growers begin the harvest, the sweet potatoes are first dug to bring the roots to the top of the soil. Then, they're either gathered mechanically or manually and transported to a processing shed where the unwashed sweet potato is cured in a climate-controlled room for several weeks. The curing process allows the skins to toughen and scratches to repair. Additionally, it gives the sugars time to develop. After the curing process, the potatoes are spray-washed and placed on a conveyor belt for further inspection. Workers line both sides of the belt and sort the sweet potatoes by grade.

They're then ready for boxing in forty-pound lots for shipment to the market. Brokers, such as Jason Bell, owner of Tater Man, Inc., buy the sweet potatoes directly from the growers and then sell them to retailers such as grocery stores. As a young boy, Jason was introduced to sweet potato farming by the farming family that raised him. After Jason reached adulthood and was trying to find his career path, he saw an opportunity to buy sweet potatoes from growers and sell to retailers. During harvest season, Jason and his team visits the sweet potato farms frequently to perform quality checks on the product.

Storage

Mature, cured sweet potatoes should not be refrigerated. Stored in a cool dark area, the sweet potatoes will last for many weeks. Discard sweet potatoes with soft spots.

Uses

If you love to eat sweet potatoes, but never cook them because you don't know how, we need to remedy that. The easiest, and most common method is baking. Here are a few tips for preparing sweet potatoes:

Baked: For softer skins, wrap in aluminum foil. For firmer skins that dry out and take on a more brittle texture, don't wrap in foil. I don't pierce the sweet potatoes with a fork prior to baking, but you can if you want to speed up the cooking time a little. A longer cooking time gives the sugars more time to develop; therefore, I choose not to pierce. Bake at 400°F for about one hour or until soft.

Roasted: Cut the sweet potatoes into sizes ranging from wedges to diced, peeled or unpeeled. Toss with cooking oil, herbs, and spices to suit your taste. Roast at 400°F for 30 minutes to 1 hour, depending on size. Roasting on high heat lets the sweet potato get a crispy outside and creamy inside.

Deep fried: Drop pieces of sweet potato in a large amount of 350°F oil. Fry until brown. Remove and drain on a rack. Salt while still hot.

Pan fried: Heat small amount cooking oil in a cast-iron skillet over medium heat. When hot, add diced or thinly sliced sweet potatoes. Flip the potatoes over when browned on one side. Cook until both sides are browned.

Microwave: A whole, middle-sized sweet potato cooks in the microwave in about 6 minutes. Sweet potato chips cook in approximately 3 minutes. It's important to follow manufacturer recommendations for microwave cooking. They all have varying degrees of wattage and cook differently.

Raw: Use grated raw sweet potatoes the same way you would carrots: slaw, cookies, cakes, etc.

Purée: I recommend peeling a baked sweet potato and mashing the flesh to get purée. Boiled sweet potatoes are less flavorful than baked. Plan ahead for lots of baking by freezing the whole baked sweet potato. Remove from the freezer, thaw, and peel when ready to use. Add purée to all types of batters: bread, pancakes, waffles, cakes, cupcakes, muffins, cookies.

Soups and stews: Add cubed sweet potato along with, or in place of, carrots.

Mashed: Season purée with butter, sweet or savory herbs, spices, syrup, and extracts.

Steamed: Peel and slice sweet potatoes. Place in a steamer basket or a microwave with a steam sensor. Steam until tender.

Boiled: Cover peeled and cubed sweet potato with water. Cover and boil over medium heat until tender. Drain and season. Serve cubed or mashed.

Demographics and Economics

The demand for sweet potatoes is on the rise globally and in the United States. Increased demand results in increased production. Each year, more than 105 million metric tons are produced globally with 95 percent of that production occurring in developing countries. The US sweet potato production has increased from 13.8 million hundredweight in 2000 to 29.6 million hundredweight in 2014. Growing consumer demand may be due to the increased promotion of sweet potatoes' health benefits. Per capita consumption in 2014 was 7.5 pounds. Sweet potatoes are suited to the southern climate of the United States and are grown in several states. North Carolina has led the nation in sweet potato production since 1971 and in 2014 produced 53 percent of sweet potatoes grown in the country. In addition to the valuable nutritional aspects of sweet potatoes, they're a commodity with significant economic impact.

A number of trade organizations, councils, and commissions promote production and consumption, educate consumers, support farmers, and collect data on sweet potatoes. The existence of these organizations underscores the importance and vitality of sweet potatoes both as a food source and a commodity. These organizations include:

- The United States Sweet Potato Council
- California Sweet Potato Council
- Louisiana Sweet Potato Commission
- Mississippi Sweet Potato Council
- North Carolina Sweet Potato Commission
- International Potato Center
- Contact information for the organizations is listed in the Resource section (page 147).

Varieties

Dozens of sweet potato varieties exist. Some are more suitable to particular environments and soil conditions than others. Skin colors range from tan to pink to orange to purple. Flesh colors range from creamy white/yellow to orange to purple. Varying amounts of sugar cause some varieties to taste sweeter than others.

Life Cycle of a Sweet Potato

Sweet potatoes are mechanically unearthed. From this point, they can be separated from the vine and harvested manually or mechanically.

They grow in clusters.

Note the different sizes.

Doug Griffin inspects sweet potatoes prior to the harvest.

Some farmers harvest sweet potatoes mechanically. The sweet potatoes all go in bins and get sorted at the processing shed.

Bins of potatoes are harvested with many more still on the ground.

Off to the processing house.

Carter and Sons Farms' processing shed.

The sweet potatoes are spray washed.

The cleaned sweet potatoes start the inspection process.

The conveyor belt is loaded and ready for workers to sort premium from culls.

Sorting.

After cleaning and sorting, sweet potatoes are cured in a temperature-controlled environment for several weeks.

A front loader is used to move forty-pound boxes of cured sweet potatoes ready for market.

Lots of activity in the sweet potato shed during harvest season.

Freshly picked and washed sweet potatoes have delicate skins. Curing toughens the skins and allows the sugars to develop.

Sweet Potatoes and Me

I've been around sweet potatoes my whole life. My parents weren't big sweet potato consumers but my grandparents certainly were. They would store sweet potatoes under straw and take them out as they needed them. My mother spoke of having nothing but a sweet potato in her lunch pail when she was in school. At least for a period of time, her school didn't serve lunches and occasionally a sweet potato was the best Granny could muster up for her lunch. On the surface, that seems sad. But, the more I learn about the powerhouse nutrition of the sweet potato, my attitude changes. It's sad that my mother and grandparents didn't live to fully appreciate all the goodness packed into a sweet potato. For the most part, they viewed a meal consisting solely of sweet potatoes as affirmation of their poor economic status. I wish they had lived long enough to understand the nutritional value of sweet potatoes.

My grandmother baked sweet potatoes often. She'd scrub them down good and place them in an oblong baking pan she called a baker. They were served hot and plenty of butter was passed around to slather all over the orange flesh. Leftovers were kept in the safe. Many times, a cold baked sweet potato served as an afternoon snack for them. If several were leftover, Granny would fry up cornbread and another vegetable to accompany sweet potatoes and that became a complete supper. There was always a sweet potato pie on her Thanksgiving table, never pumpkin.

My love for sweet potatoes developed well into my adulthood. As a child, I enjoyed candied sweet potatoes (we called them yams), which are sweet potatoes cooked with tons of butter, brown sugar, and cinnamon. However, an unfortunate sweet potato incident when I was early elementary school age created an aversion that lasted decades. I was in the kitchen with my grandmother as she cooked candied yams. Her new saltshaker on the kitchen table caught my attention. Apparently, the salt caught my attention too, because I shook some into the palm of my hand and ate it. Granny saw me doing me this and wisely advised me to stop because "the salt will dry up your blood and make you sick." Instead of heeding her warning,

I slid under the kitchen table and continued with my salt-licking expedition. She warned me again about getting sick, it was as though I were addicted. I couldn't put the saltshaker down.

Photo by Sam Garvin

She pulled the candied yams out of the oven and went on and on about how good they smelled and how pretty they looked. She wanted me to have a bite as soon as they cooled down a "speck."

Granny might have been wrong about salt drying up my blood, but she was certainly right about the salt making me sick. The thought of overly sweet and heavily buttered candied yams hitting my stomach was more than I could bear. I had two choices; either own up to the fact that I disobeyed her and spare the mouthful of candied yams coming my way, or try to fake my way out of this horrible situation and hope for the best when sugar and fat hit my queasy belly. I opted for the latter.

Big mistake. BIG mistake.

I vomited for what seemed like an eternity. I threw up food I hadn't eaten yet—futuristic throw up. Well, I couldn't eat anything that resembled sweet potatoes for the next few decades.

Luckily, my sweet potato aversion ended. I now eat sweet potatoes regularly and prefer them to white potatoes. I don't think I ever fessed up to my grandmother. Surely, she knew that I disobeyed her. I supposed she figured the punishment I bestowed upon myself was more than enough. The sweet potato industry should be mad at her. Just imagine all the sweet potatoes I would have consumed if I didn't have a thirty-year hiatus.

TJ
1809
Sea Kale

Chapter 1

FALL

Fall is the season Southerners look forward to with great anticipation. It offers mild weather in contrast to the oppressive heat and humidity of Deep South summers. We can finally open our doors and step outside without being drenched in sweat. While the days are still warm, the humidity is noticeably less and the evenings are cool. After many months of uncomfortable weather, we finally hit a point where the weather is tolerable. Our complaining, moaning, and groaning about our weather-related misery lessens. It doesn't subside, mind you. We're still complaining, but the frequency is less.

Fall used to signal the start of the school year. Nowadays, many schools start in August, but school never started for me before Labor Day. Many factors influenced this, but prominent among them was the fact that our schools in the Deep South weren't air conditioned. My first time in an air conditioned classroom was in college. We dreaded the hot classrooms and knew we had six weeks of misery. Each classroom was equipped with a big floor fan, which always seem to point at the teacher's desk. All the classrooms had large banks of windows that were left open and we lived for the cooling breezes that occasionally drifted through. Open burning was allowed and the janitor always had a fire going to burn limbs, paper, and trash. I loved the smell of a wood fire then just as I do now. Between the smell of the wood fire blowing in through the open windows and the aroma of yeast rolls and hamburger soup wafting from the kitchen, it's a wonder I kept my mind on schoolwork.

The start of school means the start of football. In the Deep South, that means the start of Southeastern Conference (SEC) football, which is an athletic conference for fourteen college teams. SEC football is serious business to the fans. Team loyalties are fierce and usually generational. My home state of Alabama is the setting for the mighty rivalry that exists between the University of Alabama and Auburn University. Any baby born in the state of Alabama has their allegiance to one of the teams declared by their parents before they're allowed to leave the hospital—something akin to an arranged marriage. As serious as folks are about SEC football, they're just as serious about game day food. Whether the game is enjoyed at home or tailgating at the stadium, the menu receives attention. Game day food is a *thing*.

Halloween, in my day, was simplistic by today's standards. My parents rarely bought Halloween costumes for us. If they did, it was a simple, inexpensive one-piece outfit with a plastic mask that obscured your view and made your face sweat. Most of the time, we had to scrounge around and make up costumes from things we found at home. I usually resorted to a ghost made by cutting holes in an old sheet, two for eyes and one for mouth, or I went as a hobo by wearing some of my father's old, worn-out clothes, and smudging black charcoal on my face to resemble a beard. Today, many families gather beforehand and share Halloween party food before taking their children out in elaborately designed costumes.

November hosts the grandest of food-related holidays: Thanksgiving. Families come together to share a meal and give thanks for their many blessings. Some families stick to a traditional menu of turkey, dressing and gravy, sweet potato casserole, and desserts. *Oh, the desserts!* Some families adopt a contemporary approach and offer foods far removed from a traditional Thanksgiving meal. Either way, the day is all about food, family, and gratitude. Thanksgiving has managed to escape the commercialization associated with almost all American holidays. I pray it stays that way.

FALL RECIPES

Cranberry Glazed Sweet Potatoes
5
Sweet Potato Casserole with Pecan Oatmeal Crumble Topping
6
Apple Cider Braised Boston Butt with Sweet Potato Mash
8
Ground Beef, Sweet Potato, and Collard Skillet Dinner
12
Sweet Potato Pie with Vanilla Meringue
15
Maple Sweet Potato Granola Bars
16
Sweet Potato Pear Cranberry Scones with Maple Ginger Glaze
18
Apple Cider Brined Chicken and Sweet Potato Skillet
21
Sweet Potato Chipotle Hummus
23
Apple Sweet Potato Fried Pies
26
Sweet Potato Apple Butter
29
Apple Butter Twice-Baked Sweet Potatoes
30
Sweet Potato Muffins with Cranberry Pear Filling
33
Pecan and Sweet Potato Pie
35
Sweet Potato Pie with Gingersnap Cookie Crust and Bourbon Whipped Cream
36

CRANBERRY GLAZED SWEET POTATOES

Preheat oven to 350°F
Yield: 4 servings

Candied yams were a staple at Thanksgiving Dinner at our house. Canned sweet potatoes, marketed as yams, were used. The sweet potatoes were drained from the syrup, thrown into a casserole dish, topped with gobs of brown sugar and butter, dusted with cinnamon, and baked until bubbling, after which they were topped with marshmallows that were baked until toasted. I loved that dish then and still do today. It served as my inspiration for this dish, starting with fresh sweet potatoes instead of relying on the canned product. Tart cranberries are a nice balance to the sweetness of brown sugar and make an excellent glaze for sweet potatoes.

Cranberry glaze:

½ cup unsalted butter
½ cup brown sugar, firmly packed
2 tablespoons vanilla extract or bourbon
1 teaspoon ground cinnamon
½ teaspoon ground ginger
½ teaspoon kosher salt
1 cup fresh cranberries

Sweet potatoes:

3 medium raw sweet potatoes, peeled and cut in ¼-inch-thick rounds
1 tablespoon butter

Make the glaze

Add all ingredients except cranberries to a small saucepan over medium-low heat. Stir until brown sugar has melted. Add cranberries and simmer for 5 minutes. Set aside.

Make the potatoes

Arrange sweet potatoes in a buttered 9-inch cast-iron skillet in a circular pattern, slightly overlapping.

Strain cranberries from glaze and set aside. Drizzle glaze over sweet potatoes in skillet. Cover and cook at 350°F for 45 minutes or until sweet potatoes are tender. Baste occasionally during cooking.

Remove cover and scatter cooked cranberries over sweet potatoes. Place back in oven, uncovered, for an additional 10 minutes.

SWEET POTATO CASSEROLE WITH PECAN OATMEAL CRUMBLE TOPPING

Preheat oven to 350°F
Yield: 8 servings

Thanksgiving Dinner without sweet potato casserole is like trying to pronounce Thanksgiving without vowels: thnksfvng. Oh, you'd eventually figure it out, but it's just not right and a key component is missing. My recipe has a lot of ingredients, but nothing exotic. It comes together quickly. To make ahead, assemble and store in refrigerator until ready to bake. The hardest thing about this casserole is deciding if it's served as a side or dessert. Why worry? Serve it as both.

Filling:

8 ounces cream cheese, softened
¼ cup (½ stick) butter, softened
½ cup light brown sugar, firmly packed
4 medium to large sweet potatoes, baked and peeled
½ cup half-and-half or cream
¼ teaspoon fresh grated nutmeg
½ teaspoon ground cinnamon
1 teaspoon vanilla
1 tablespoon honey

Topping:

½ cup pecans, chopped
½ cup light brown sugar, firmly packed
¼ cup (½ stick) butter, cold and diced
½ cup quick cooking oatmeal, uncooked
¼ teaspoon freshly grated nutmeg
½ teaspoon cinnamon
¼ teaspoon salt

Make the filling

Cream softened cream cheese and butter until light and fluffy. Add brown sugar and cream until smooth. Throw in cooked, peeled sweet potatoes. Mix until smooth. Add half-and-half or cream, nutmeg, cinnamon, vanilla, and honey. Mix. Taste for sweetness and spices. If it's just right, pour into a greased 8 x 8 baking pan. Smooth out the top. This stuff tastes good enough to eat as is, but hold on to your hats. We're going to make it even better.

Make the topping

Add topping ingredients to a bowl. Smoosh it all up until it resembles coarse cornmeal. (I use my clean hands. They're the best smooshers I own.) Sprinkle it all over the top of the filling. If some happens to fall off on your counter as you're sprinkling, you're required to eat it. Bake at 350°F for 45 minutes or until the top has browned and the filling is bubbly. Let sit for 5 minutes, if you can wait that long, before serving. If you can't wait 5 minutes, be very careful that you don't burn your tonsils. This stuff is piping hot!

SWEET TIPS

Brown sugar is granulated sugar and molasses. Make your own by adding 1 tablespoon to 1 cup of sugar. Stir with a fork until well incorporated. Store in an airtight container.

APPLE CIDER BRAISED BOSTON BUTT
WITH SWEET POTATO MASH

Preheat oven to 250°F
Yield: 6–8 servings

Apple, pork, and sweet potatoes are a surefire combination. Braise a seasoned Boston butt pork roast in a vegetable and apple cider mixture and serve over apple cider–kissed mashed sweet potatoes that get a little zing from cayenne pepper. Slow-simmer the pork until it's falling apart and tender. Shred it and add back some of the cooking liquid for additional flavor.

Rub:

1 tablespoon brown sugar, firmly packed
1 tablespoon kosher salt
1 tablespoon dry barbeque seasoning mix

Boston butt:

1 boneless 4-lb. Boston butt pork roast (average size)
1–2 tablespoons yellow mustard
2 sweet onions, peeled and sliced
3 carrots, cut in thirds, crosswise
2 celery stalks, halved
7–8 garlic cloves, smashed and peeled
1½ cups apple cider
½ cup apple cider vinegar

Make the Rub

Mix together and set aside.

Prep the butt

Score fat cap, but do not remove. Coat Boston butt with mustard outside and inside the cavity. Repeat with rub. Set aside.

Make the butt

Add onions, carrots, celery, and garlic to a cast-iron Dutch oven or a large, heavy-bottomed kettle. Place seasoned Boston butt on top of vegetables. Pour apple cider and apple cider vinegar over pork roast.

Cover and cook on 250°F for 5 hours or until internal temperature of the meat reaches 190°F. Baste occasionally while cooking.

Take roast from Dutch oven, remove fat cap. Shred roast with two forks and place in a bowl. Add enough pan juices to the pork to moisten. Taste for seasonings and adjust as needed. Serve on top of mashed potatoes (recipe below).

SWEET POTATO MASH

Preheat oven to 350°F

Yield: 4–6 servings

4 medium sweet potatoes, baked
4 tablespoons butter
4 tablespoons apple cider
⅛ teaspoon ground cayenne pepper
¼ teaspoon kosher salt

Bake sweet potatoes until tender. Remove from oven.

When cool enough to handle, peel sweet potatoes and place in a large bowl. Add remaining ingredients and mash until smooth. Reheat if necessary.

Sweet Potatoes are for Endurance Athletes . . .

In 2008, Marcia Garvin rescued a little Jack Russell terrier mix and named her Winter. True to the breed, Winter needed lots of exercise and loved to run outside every chance she got. Running spaces were limited in their townhome complex though, so Marcia started jogging with Winter. As Marcia built endurance, jogging became running, and the length of the runs increased. Within a year, Marcia realized her endurance was greater than Winter's. She'd outrun her little Jack Russell terrier.

Marcia is my daughter and our family's version of Forrest Gump. She just felt like running so she ran, and ran, and ran. She's finished thirty-one marathons, one full Iron Man Triathlon, five half Iron Man Triathlons, six 50k (approximately 32 miles) trail races, and one 50-mile trail race. Additionally, she's completed two 280-mile charity bike rides from Ft. Myers, Florida, to Key West, Florida. In the process, she's dropped about eighty-five pounds. Needless to say, her cardiovascular health is impeccable.

Marcia includes sweet potato in her regular menu plans. They have a low glycemic index, which means the carbohydrates are easily digested and absorbed gradually. Slow absorption of carbohydrates is critically important to endurance athletes as carbohydrates are the primary fuel source for athletic muscles and provide sustained energy.

Marcia continues her lifestyle as an endurance athlete and takes Winter for runs with her when possible. (Winter's limit is about seven or eight miles.) For Marcia's longer runs, she enjoys running with friends who share the same endurance and enthusiasm.

Winter is one lucky pup that she was adopted by Marcia. With a new passion for running and overall endurance, Marcia is healthy and happy. Her enthusiasm is rooted in a desire to exercise her doggie.

The burning question is: "Who rescued who?"

GROUND BEEF, SWEET POTATO, AND COLLARD SKILLET DINNER

Preheat oven to 400°F
Yield: 6 servings

A healthy, nutrient-dense one pot meal fits the needs of endurance athletes. It meets their nutritional requirements and makes several meals that can easily be reheated and are ready when needed. Roasting vegetables before adding to the skillet helps develop the natural sugars and provides more flavor.

3 carrots, chopped
1 sweet potato, chopped
1 cup cherry tomatoes
2 tablespoons coconut oil, divided
salt and pepper to taste
2 medium sweet onions, chopped
3 cloves garlic, minced
1 (16-ounce) bag collard greens, chopped
2 cups chicken stock
1 lb. grass-fed ground beef

Cover a large baking sheet with aluminum foil and coat with a nonstick cooking spray. Add carrots, sweet potato, and cherry tomatoes. Drizzle with coconut oil. Sprinkle salt and pepper. Toss until coated. Spread vegetables to a single layer. Place in a 400°F preheated oven. Bake for 45 minutes or until they have started to brown.

In a large skillet, sauté onions in remaining coconut oil. Cook until tender, stirring occasionally.

Add garlic and cook 5 minutes longer.

Add chopped collard greens and chicken stock. Stir. Cover and simmer for 30 minutes, stirring occasionally, until collard greens have cooked down and are tender. When done, remove the cover and let most of the remaining liquid cook out.

Add ground beef and cook until all the pink is gone. Stir in roasted vegetables. Taste for seasoning and serve warm.

SWEET TIPS

Use ginger along with nutmeg to soften the "in your face" boldness of nutmeg.

SWEET POTATO PIE WITH VANILLA MERINGUE

Preheat oven to 350°F
Yield: 1 (9-inch) pie

My grandmother never made a pumpkin pie in her life, but she turned out a boat load of sweet potato pies. It was a standard at Thanksgiving, along with pecan pies and pound cake. She never cooked a turkey, either, so a picture of a Thanksgiving meal at her house didn't resemble the iconic Norman Rockwell painting. I grew up thinking a pumpkin pie must be something magical and special. Many years later, I learned the most special pie was the one that had been on our Thanksgiving table all along.

Filling:

4 sweet potatoes, baked and skin removed
5 ounces evaporated milk
1 teaspoon vanilla extract
1 teaspoon ground cinnamon
½ teaspoon ginger
¼ teaspoon nutmeg
¼ teaspoon cloves
½ teaspoon kosher salt
4 tablespoons butter, softened
½ cup granulated sugar
½ cup brown sugar
2 large eggs
9-inch unbaked pie crust

Meringue:

3 egg whites, room temperature
¼ teaspoon cream of tartar
½ teaspoon vanilla
¾ cup white sugar

Make the filling

Mash sweet potatoes and stir in milk, vanilla, cinnamon, ginger, nutmeg, cloves, and salt. Set aside.

Cream butter and sugars until smooth. Add eggs and beat until light. Add sweet potato mixture and beat until well incorporated. Pour into pie crust. Bake in a 350°F preheated oven for 1 hour or until a knife inserted in the center of the pie filling comes out clean.

Make the meringue

Beat egg whites, cream of tartar, and vanilla until frothy. Gradually add sugar, beating until mixture forms stiff peaks.

Cover warm pie all the way to the edges with meringue.

Place pie under broiler until meringue browns slightly. Watch it carefully. Don't get distracted—meringue burns easily. Burned meringue hurts your feelings.

Remove immediately. Cool completely before cutting.

MAPLE SWEET POTATO GRANOLA BARS

Preheat oven to 350°F
Yield: 1 (11x16) pan

For breakfast on the run or a snack, this granola can't be beaten. Fruits, nuts, sweet potato, and oats create a nutritional powerhouse in a delicious package. You need a large bowl for mixing. Don't cut yourself short. I use the one I use for Thanksgiving dressing that's dishpan size. Give yourself plenty of stirring room to make sure all the oatmeal mixture is well coated with the liquid mixture.

2 cups quick-cooking oatmeal
1 cup shredded coconut, sweetened
1 cup pecans, roughly chopped
1 cup dried cranberries, sweetened
1 cup dried banana chips
8 tablespoons butter
½ cup pure maple syrup
¼ cup brown sugar (light or dark)
½ cup creamy peanut butter
1 cup sweet potato, peeled, cooked, and mashed
1 tablespoon ground cinnamon

Place oatmeal, coconut, and pecans in a large sheet pan sprayed with a nonstick cooking spray. Stir together lightly. Place in preheated oven for about 20 minutes or until lightly browned. Remove from oven and pour into a large bowl. Add cranberries and banana chips. Keep oven on.

Place butter, syrup, brown sugar, peanut butter, sweet potato, and cinnamon in a medium saucepan. Heat over medium heat, stirring frequently, until all ingredients have dissolved and mixture is smooth. Pour over oats mixture and stir until all the ingredients are coated well.

Spray a medium sheet pan (approximately 11 x 14 inches) with a nonstick cooking spray. Spread granola mixture evenly in pan. If mixture sticks, spray nonstick cooking spray on top of granola.

Bake in preheated oven for 20 minutes or until mixture browns.

Cool completely in pan before cutting.

SWEET POTATO PEAR CRANBERRY SCONES WITH MAPLE GINGER GLAZE

Preheat oven to 450°F
Yield: 8–12 scones

I tried to slam as many fall flavors as possible into one recipe. Sweet potatoes, dried sweetened cranberries, pears, maple syrup, cinnamon, and ginger all found their way into this flavorful, flaky, and delightful scone. I use Bosc pears because they hold up a little better for baking, but any soft cooking pear will work. Start your day with one for breakfast or pack them for tailgating and parties.

Scones:

2½ cups self-rising flour, plus additional
1 teaspoon ground cinnamon
½ teaspoon ground ginger
½ cup unsalted butter, cubed and chilled
½ cup dried cranberries, sweetened
1 Bosc pear, peeled, cored, and diced
1 medium sweet potato, baked and skin removed
1 cup buttermilk
2 tablespoons pure maple syrup
cooking oil or melted butter for the tops

Glaze:

2 cups powdered sugar
1 teaspoon ground ginger
1 tablespoon maple syrup
2–3 tablespoons buttermilk

Make the scones

Add flour, cinnamon, and ginger to a large bowl and stir lightly. Cut or rub in butter until the flour resembles coarse meal. Stir in cranberries and pear.

Add sweet potato flesh, buttermilk, and maple syrup to a small bowl and stir until mixed.

Add sweet potato mixture to dry ingredients. Stir with a large wooden spoon until well incorporated. The mixture should be wet and sticky.

Turn the mixture out onto a floured surface. Add more flour and gently work it into the dough until it's no longer sticky and holds its shape.

Form the dough into a 1-inch-thick disc and cut into 8 wedges, or form it into a 1-inch-thick rectangle and cut 6 squares of equal size and halve the squares for a total of 12 pieces.

Spray a baking sheet with a nonstick cooking spray or cover with a baking mat. Place dough on sheet, 1 inch apart. Brush tops with cooking oil or melted butter.

Bake in a 450°F preheated oven for 20 minutes or until the tops are golden brown. Remove to a cooling rack and cool for 10 minutes then glaze.

Make the glaze

Whisk until smooth. Drizzle over scones.

SWEET TIPS

Maple syrup has different levels of flavor intensity. Read the description on the bottle and pick the one that best describes your desired level of maple-y flavor.

SWEET TIPS

Substitute one onion cut in fourths for shallot.

APPLE CIDER BRINED CHICKEN AND SWEET POTATO SKILLET

Preheat oven to 400°F
Yield: 4 servings

This delicious dish is a skillet meal of apple cider brined chicken with sweet potatoes and shallots served with an apple cider pan sauce atop the chicken. A brining liquid will infuse flavors into the meat and help keep it moist. To make a brining liquid, you need a balance between sweet and salty. Outside of that, throw in any flavor in the way of aromatics, herbs, or spices that suit your fancy. This recipe requires advance planning, but the technique is simple and the results are outstanding. Lemons or common limes can be substituted for key limes, which I used because I had them on hand. They're little bitty tiny limes, easy to find in Florida grocery stores. Substitute one regular sliced lemon or lime for the key limes listed.

Brine:

2 cups apple cider
3 key limes, halved
1 sprig fresh rosemary
4–5 fresh sage leaves
⅓ cup kosher salt
½ cup brown sugar
1 bay leaf
10 peppercorns
3 garlic cloves, peeled and smashed
1 sweet onion, peeled and sliced
2 cups water
4 chicken thighs, bone in and skin on

Skillet dish:

2 medium-sized sweet potatoes, peeled and cut in 1-inch cubes
2 medium shallots, peeled and halved
1 tablespoon fresh sage, finely chopped
1 teaspoon fresh rosemary, finely chopped
cooking oil
½ cup all-purpose flour
1 teaspoon kosher salt
¼ teaspoon ground black pepper
¼ teaspoon garlic powder
4 brined chicken thighs

Pan gravy:

1 tablespoon grease from skillet
1 tablespoon seasoned flour
1 cup apple cider
1 tablespoon deli-style mustard

Continued on page 22

Make the brine

Place all ingredients, except chicken, in a saucepan. Heat to a gentle boil, stirring occasionally. Remove from heat and let cool to room temperature.

After the brine is cool, place chicken pieces in a gallon storage bag placed inside a bowl. (I had a brine bag spring a leak and brine the entire inside surface of my refrigerator. A bowl will save cleanup if that happens.) Carefully pour cooled brining liquid over chicken pieces. Store in refrigerator for 4 hours. After 4 hours, remove chicken from brine.

Make the skillet dish

Place sweet potatoes, shallots, sage, rosemary, and 1 tablespoon cooking oil in a large bowl. Stir until coated. Set aside.

Add flour, kosher salt, ground black pepper, and garlic powder in a storage bag. Reserve 1 tablespoon of seasoned flour. Add chicken pieces one at a time and shake until coated with seasoned flour. Set chicken aside.

Heat a large cast-iron skillet on medium-high heat. Coat the bottom with cooking oil. When the skillet is hot, add dredged chicken pieces, skin side down. Cook on one side about 2 minutes or until light golden brown. Flip pieces over.

Scatter sweet potato and shallot mixture in the skillet, leaving the tops of the chicken uncovered.

Place skillet in preheated oven and cook for 45 minutes or until the internal temperature of the chicken is 165°F and the skin is crispy and brown.

Remove from oven. Transfer chicken and vegetables to a platter.

Make the pan gravy

Drain grease from skillet, leaving 1 tablespoon. Don't dare discard all the crunchies left in the pan.

Place the skillet on medium-high heat. Stir in reserved seasoned flour. Stir continuously until all grease is absorbed. Once the flour is brown, whisk in apple cider and mustard until the gravy is thickened. Remove from heat and serve immediately over chicken.

SWEET POTATO CHIPOTLE HUMMUS

Yield: approximately 4 cups

Sweetness from sweet potato and smokiness from chipotle make this hummus a winner. Make it for your next tailgate party. Use canned chipotle peppers in a tomato-based sauce called adobo. Serve with pita chips or fresh vegetables for dipping.

1 medium sweet potato, baked, cooled, and peeled
1 (15-ounce) can chickpeas, drained
3 tablespoons olive oil, plus extra if needed
3 tablespoons tahini
3 garlic cloves
1 chipotle pepper
1 tablespoon adobo sauce
1 tablespoon chili pepper
juice of 1 lime
½ teaspoon kosher salt

Add all ingredients to a food processor and process until smooth, adding additional olive oil as needed. For less heat, remove the seeds from the chipotle pepper.

Sweet Potatoes Are for Cast Iron Enthusiasts . . .

My sister, Kathy Anderson, didn't inherit my love of cooking. Her husband is the chief cook and bottle washer around their house. Cast-iron cooking implements were regular fixtures in our grandmothers' and mother's kitchens but they never captured her attention. A few years ago, Kathy had a renewed interest in cast iron. Her interest quickly turned into an obsession and her collection steadily grew. Along with Kathy's interest in cast iron came a strange and peculiar thing: she figured out she loves to cook in cast iron in addition to collecting.

But she hasn't run her husband out of the kitchen yet. Even though he still cooks the majority of their meals, sweet potatoes are well-suited to cast iron cooking and earned a spot in Kathy's recipe portfolio.

APPLE SWEET POTATO FRIED PIES

Preheat oven to 350°F
Yield: 20 fried pies

Traditional southern fried pies are made with a filling of dried apples reconstituted by adding water and sugar. They're simmered until tender. The filling is placed in pastry crusts or biscuits and quickly deep fried. For this recipe, sweet potatoes, fresh apples, raisins, and nuts are added for extra flavor, resulting in an updated version of a favorite classic. The use of cast iron twice in this recipe appeals to those who consider it their cooking vessel of choice.

Filling:

¾ cup brown sugar, firmly packed
1 teaspoon ground cinnamon
¼ teaspoon ground ginger
¼ teaspoon ground nutmeg
½ teaspoon kosher salt
2 medium-sized sweet potatoes, baked, peeled, and sliced in rounds
2 large Granny Smith apples, peeled, cored, and sliced in rounds
1 cup pecans, chopped
½ cup raisins
3 tablespoons unsalted butter, cubed

Fried pies:

½ cup granulated sugar
1 teaspoon ground cinnamon
1 package (10-count) refrigerator biscuits
sweet potato apple filling
water
cooking oil

Make the filling

Stir together brown sugar, cinnamon, ginger, nutmeg, and salt. Set aside.

In a well-greased 9-inch cast-iron skillet, layer half the sweet potato and apple slices. Top with half the pecans and raisins. Sprinkle half the sugar mixture.

Repeat with remaining ingredients. Dot with butter cubes. Cover and bake in a 350°F preheated oven for 20 minutes or until sugar has dissolved and apples are tender. Remove from oven and stir.

Make fried pies

Add sugar and cinnamon to a small bowl. Stir and set aside.

Cut each biscuit in half and roll into a circle. Place a small amount of filling in the center of each biscuit. Dip your finger into water and moisten around the outside of the biscuit.

Fold biscuit in half and crimp the edges with a fork.

Heat 2 inches of cooking oil to 350°F in a cast-iron kettle or a large, heavy-bottomed cooking vessel.

Working in batches, drop the pie into the hot oil for about 1 minute or until brown on one side. Flip and repeat with the other side.

Remove to a wire rack. While still hot, roll the pie in a sugar/cinnamon mixture.

SWEET POTATO APPLE BUTTER

Yield: 4–6 pints

Sweet potato apple butter isn't just for smearing on biscuits and toasts, although both uses are mighty fine. Use it as a topping for oatmeal. Heated, it makes a fancy topping for vanilla ice cream. Your waffles and pancakes will love it.

4 medium-sized sweet potatoes, peeled and cut in chunks
3 medium Granny Smith apples, peeled, cored, and quartered
1 lemon, halved and seeds removed
½ cup brown sugar, firmly packed
2 teaspoons ground cinnamon
1 teaspoon ground ginger
1 teaspoon ground nutmeg
½ teaspoon kosher salt
½ cup apple cider

Place all ingredients in a slow cooker in the order listed. Cook on low overnight, up to 12 hours.

The next morning, or after 12 hours and a good night's rest, remove the lemon. Purée the sweet potato/apple mixture with an immersion blender. Keep cooking, uncovered, until desired consistency is reached. If a smoother texture is desired, add additional apple cider.

Taste for sweetness and spices. If it's not sweet enough to suit your taste, add additional brown sugar while the mixture is still hot and the sugar will melt. As an option, sweeten with honey.

Ladle into containers and store in the refrigerator for up to 2 weeks or freeze for up to 6 months.

APPLE BUTTER TWICE-BAKED SWEET POTATOES

Preheat oven to 400°F
Yield: 4 servings

Fall harvest is here for sure if we're talking about sweet potatoes and apples. Mix a little bit of apple butter with baked sweet potato flesh, stuff the potatoes, and pop them back in the oven.

2 medium-sized sweet potatoes
2 tablespoons apple butter
2 tablespoons melted butter
ground cinnamon

Wrap the sweet potatoes in aluminum foil. Bake at 400°F for an hour or until soft.

When they're cool enough to handle, remove the aluminum foil and split them in half lengthwise. With a spoon, gently scoop out the flesh, leaving a thin layer in the shell, and put the flesh in a bowl. Add apple butter and melted butter. Stir until smooth.

Refill the potato shells with the mixture. Lightly sprinkle with ground cinnamon. Place back in the oven for 10 minutes or until reheated.

Serve warm.

Wilton

SWEET POTATO MUFFINS WITH CRANBERRY PEAR FILLING

Preheat oven to 400°F
Yield: 12 large muffins

If sweet potato muffins aren't enough to get folks' attention, throw in some cranberry pear cobbler–like filling and you will be their best friend forever. What a great way to start a day and a friendship. Make these the night before and dream about them for breakfast. Enjoy them for an afternoon snack and get some pep back in your step. Make up a batch any time you need a reminder of just how wonderful fall is.

Filling:

½ cup unsalted butter
½ brown sugar, firmly packed
2 tablespoons vanilla extract or bourbon
½ teaspoon ground cinnamon
½ teaspoon ground ginger
½ teaspoon kosher salt
1 cup fresh cranberries
2 Bosc pears, cored and diced, peeled or unpeeled

Muffins:

1½ cups self-rising flour
⅓ cup brown sugar, firmly packed
1 teaspoon ground cinnamon
1 teaspoon ground ginger
½ teaspoon ground nutmeg
1 cup buttermilk
½ teaspoon baking soda
¼ cup cooking oil (I used canola)
2 large eggs
1 baked sweet potato, peeled and mashed

Make the filling

Melt butter and sugar in a small saucepan on medium heat, stirring frequently. Add remaining ingredients. Bring to a boil and cook for 10 minutes, stirring frequently. Set aside.

Make muffins

Add flour, brown sugar, cinnamon, ginger, and nutmeg to a large mixing bowl. Stir.

To a medium bowl, add buttermilk and baking soda. Stir to combine. Add oil, eggs, and sweet potato and whisk to combine.

Pour wet ingredients into dry ingredients. Stir just until combined. Don't overstir.

Line a 12-cup cupcake pan with paper baking cups. Fill each baking cup ⅓ full of muffin batter. Divide fruit filling among the baking cups. Top fruit filling with remaining muffin batter.

Bake in a 400°F oven for 30 minutes. Let cool before eating. The filling needs to cool before it will set up properly. Also, you don't want to eat it piping hot and let the boiled, syrupy fruit filling hit the back of your throat. It will burn the fool out of you.

PECAN AND SWEET POTATO PIE

Preheat oven to 350°F
Yield: 1 (9-inch) pie

Pecan is my husband's favorite pie. We have a family recipe that belonged to his Aunt Bea, who was known for her pecan pies. I made a modified version of a pecan pie and added a sweet potato filling. As we say in the South, "It's fittin' to eat."

Sweet potato filling:

2 medium-sized sweet potatoes, baked and peeled
½ cup firmly packed brown sugar
2 tablespoons unsalted butter, melted
2 teaspoons vanilla extract
½ teaspoon ground cinnamon
¼ teaspoon ground nutmeg
½ teaspoon ground ginger
1 tablespoon buttermilk
9-inch pie crust

Pecan topping:

¾ cup corn syrup
2 large eggs
½ teaspoon kosher salt
1 cup pecan halves

Make sweet potato filling

Mix together all ingredients, except the pie crust. The mixture should be spreadable but not pourable. If necessary, add another tablespoon of buttermilk to attain spreadable consistency.

Spread into the bottom of the pie crust.

Make pecan topping

Whisk together corn syrup, eggs, and kosher salt. Stir in pecans. Pour over sweet potato filling. Spread pecans evenly.

Bake pie

Bake at 350°F for 45 minutes or until filling is set and the top is brown. Remove from oven and completely cool on a rack before cutting.

SWEET POTATO PIE WITH GINGERSNAP COOKIE CRUST AND BOURBON WHIPPED CREAM

Preheat oven to 350°F
Yield: 1 (9-inch) pie

Sweet potatoes and ginger are natural go-togethers, so a gingersnap cookie crust for a sweet potato pie makes good natural sense. No explanation needed for bourbon whipped cream.

Crust:

1½ cups gingersnap cookie crumbs (about 36 cookies ground in a food processor)
½ cup unsalted butter, melted and cooled

Filling:

4 sweet potatoes, baked and skin removed
5 ounces evaporated milk
1 teaspoon vanilla extract
1 teaspoon ground cinnamon
½ teaspoon ginger
¼ teaspoon nutmeg
¼ teaspoon cloves
½ teaspoon kosher salt
4 tablespoons butter, softened
½ cup granulated sugar
½ cup brown sugar
2 large eggs

Bourbon whipped cream:

1 cup heavy whipping cream, cold
1–2 tablespoons powdered sugar
½ tablespoon vanilla extract
1 tablespoon bourbon

Make crust

Mix cookie crumbs and melted butter until it resembles wet sand. Press into a 9-inch pie plate and cover the bottom and sides. Chill crust for at least 1 hour before baking. Bake in a 350°F preheated oven for 10 minutes. Remove and cool before filling.

Make the filling

Mash sweet potatoes and stir in milk, vanilla, cinnamon, ginger, nutmeg, cloves, and salt. Set aside. Cream butter and sugars until smooth. Add eggs and beat until light. Add sweet potato mixture and beat until well incorporated. Pour into gingersnap cookie crust and bake in a 350°F preheated oven for 1 hour or until a knife inserted in the center of the pie filling comes out clean.

Make the whipped cream

With electric mixer, whip cream until soft peaks form. Add sugar and whip to stiff peaks. Stir in vanilla extract and bourbon. Serve on top of pie. Garnish with whole cookies, if desired. Or just eat the cookies. Nobody's looking.

Ella

Jackson
2012

Chapter 2

WINTER

Winter is a season I looked forward to as a child with great anticipation and wonderment. I've never lived in a cold-weather climate so the anticipation of snowball fights, snowman building, sledding, snow days, and winter sports wasn't a reality. On rare occasions it snowed where I lived. If we were lucky, we could gather enough for snow ice cream and possibly enough for a few snowballs. The epicenter of my winter excitement was Christmas and all the surrounding activities. Schools would rehearse special music and plays, churches made preparations for pageants and the Christmas Story. I'd dream of the best gift I could buy or make for family members with my limited (very limited) financial resources.

It's customary today for stores to bring out their Christmas displays while we're still two or three holidays away from Christmas. The prolonged exposure to Christmas displays, decorations, and gift ideas takes away the anticipation of this beautiful, sacred holiday. Nowadays, by the time Christmas rolls around, we're all tired of it. I remember feelings of elation and sadness on Christmas morning; excitement and happiness that Christmas was finally here, yet sadness that it was over until next year.

My earliest recollection of our family Christmas tree was when I was eight years old. We had trees before then but they've escaped my memory. My eighth Christmas was when my mother jumped on the trendy bandwagon of aluminum trees with a color wheel that spun around and changed the color of the tree. Even though I was only eight, that didn't seem like a proper Christmas tree. However, since I was only eight, I didn't get a vote. At least we had a tree. I suppose that was the most important point.

A few years later, my mother announced that we would ditch the aluminum tree in favor of a real Christmas tree. *A real, live evergreen tree that looked like a Christmas tree and smelled like a Christmas tree!* That was almost more excitement than my little heart could handle. But the excitement was short-lived. The next announcement from my mother laid out her decorating plans for the beautiful evergreen: blue lights and blue satin balls. *Blue.* Not traditional Christmas colors of red, gold, or silver. Not red-and-white candy canes. Not vintage glass ornaments. Nothing but blue lights and blue satin balls.

When the tree was finally decorated, my mother couldn't have been more proud. She thought it was the most beautiful tree she'd ever laid eyes on.

"The blue just sets it off," she declared.

I tried to love that tree and its decorations. A real Christmas tree had been a dream for so long. I grabbed the end of a limb and brought my face down to it to smell its freshness. Suddenly, the evergreen tree with the unlikely decorations was beautiful. The fresh aroma of the sticky needles was almost overpowering. I forgot about blue decorations and focused on the magnificent aroma. My disappointment abated, I fell in love with the tree. My sense of smell showed me the beauty my sense of sight was unable to notice. I was saved by my nose. To this day, I can't walk past an evergreen tree without grabbing a handful of needles to sniff.

There was a time that I filled every room in my own house with a themed Christmas tree. I would spend weeks decorating and sometimes longer un-decorating. It was a lot of work but I felt it was worth the effort. Lately, I've scaled back my Christmas decorating significantly. The realization hit me that I was more interested in all the decorations than anyone else so I was creating a magnitude of extra work for myself. All our children are grown and our grandchildren live 1,400 miles away. We will, more than likely, visit them on Christmas instead of them coming to our house. So, I find myself in another phase of my life. Perhaps my days of extensive decorations are over. I find that bittersweet.

Without the hustle, bustle, and stress of decking my house with massive volumes of Christmas decorations, I'm more at peace. Christmas is the season of peace and love so my attitude is more in tune with the spirit of the season. I need to find a balance between the way I used to decorate and the way normal people decorate. It's still Christmas with one tree. Decorating fourteen trees doesn't make it any more Christmas. Intellectually, I agree. Emotionally, I still need some work.

WINTER RECIPES

A Supper of Chicken and Vegetables
42
Balsamic Glazed Sweet Potatoes and Leeks
45
Banana Sweet Potato Breakfast Bread
46
Caribbean Jerk Quinoa and Sweet Potato
51
Chicken, Potato, and Cabbage Bake
52
Chilled Strawberry Sweet Potato Soup
55
Key Lime Sweet Potato Bisque with Key Lime Cream
57
Lentil, Sweet Potato, and Chipotle Pepper Chili
58
Split Pea, Ham, and Sweet Potato Soup
61
Sweet Potato and Pear Soup
62
Sweet Potato Cake Doughnuts with Vanilla Buttermilk Glaze
64
Sweet Potato Cake with Coconut Custard Cream Filling and Buttermilk Cinnamon Glaze
67
Citrus Garlic Cornish Game Hens with Sweet Potato Cornbread Dressing
69
Sweet Potato Cornbread
71
Sweet Potato Pound Cake with Meyer Lemon Glaze
72

A SUPPER OF CHICKEN AND VEGETABLES

Preheat oven to 350°F
Yield: 4 servings

We try to visit Colonial Williamsburg as often as possible. Naturally, each visit inspires me to cook eighteenth-century style. I don't have an open hearth so I can cook authentic eighteenth-century fare, but I follow their methods of simple, seasonal, fresh ingredients. One pot is common because kitchens typically had only one source of fire. Shop owners, craftsmen, and middling farmers may own only a few cooking vessels. Cooking one-pot meals was both practical and necessary. This dish is simple enough for a busy family yet good enough to share with houseguests. This is a fine supper for a cold winter's night.

8 chicken thighs, skin on and bone in
salt and pepper or your favorite poultry seasoning
bacon grease or cooking oil
12 carrots, peeled and trimmed
2 Yukon gold potatoes, peeled and left whole
2 medium-sized sweet potatoes, peeled and left whole
1 medium sweet onion, peeled and left whole
2 celery stalks, cut in half, crosswise
½ lb. whole Brussels sprouts, trimmed and left whole
a few sprigs of fresh herbs, such as thyme, rosemary, and sage

Season both sides of chicken and set aside.

Coat the bottom of a large cooking vessel with bacon grease or oil and heat over medium-high.

When the cooking vessel is hot, add the seasoned chicken skin-side down, working in batches. Cook the chicken on each side for 3 to 4 minutes until it starts to brown. Remove the chicken and repeat with the remaining chicken.

Add carrots to the bottom of the vessel. Next, add potatoes and onion. Place celery across the top. Lay the Brussels sprouts on top, keeping them in the center. Spread the herbs on top evenly. Place the chicken on top of the vegetables in a single layer. Pour any juices from the chicken on top.

Cover and cook at 350°F for 1½ hours or until the internal temperature in the chicken reaches 165°F. If the chicken isn't browned to your liking, remove from the kettle, place on a large baking sheet, and broil before serving.

Remove herb sprigs before serving.

SWEET TIPS

Garnish with chopped green onions cut on the diagonal or chopped fresh chives.

BALSAMIC GLAZED SWEET POTATOES AND LEEKS

Preheat oven to 400°F
Yield: 4–6 servings

Leeks are a wonderful winter crop that is easily overlooked. Their popularity in Europe was noted long before we decided to sit up and take notice in the United States. The flavor reminds me of potato soup: mild with a hint of onion. Sweet potatoes and leeks complement each other. Leeks require special attention to cleaning to remove the sand and dirt. After slicing, place them in ice cold water in a large bowl so the leeks float on the top. Gently press them under the water a few times and let them sit for at least 15 minutes. Carefully skim them from the top of the water. You will see the debris sink to the bottom.

2 sweet potatoes, peeled and cut into matchsticks
2 large leeks, whites only, sliced crosswise (cleaning instructions are in the header)
2 tablespoons olive oil
1 tablespoon balsamic vinegar
salt and pepper, to taste

Place sweet potatoes and leeks on a large baking sheet covered with aluminum foil and sprayed with a nonstick cooking spray.

Add oil, vinegar, salt, and pepper to vegetables and toss until coated.

Bake 40 minutes, stirring occasionally in a preheated 400°F oven until sweet potatoes are tender. Some of the leeks get crispy, which is a bonus!

BANANA SWEET POTATO BREAKFAST BREAD

Preheat oven to 350°F
Yield: 1 loaf

This moist, tasty, quick bread made with bananas, sweet potatoes, peanuts, raisins, coconut, and warm spices will hit the spot on cold mornings. A toasted slice, along with a hot beverage, will warm your innards as you prepare for the winter's day. And if that's not enough incentive to bake a loaf of this mighty fine bread, you don't need to drag out your mixer for this. Make it ahead and slice it when you're ready for it. Freeze it and let it thaw on your countertop. You will want to make up a double batch when company's a-coming.

1 cup self-rising flour
1 teaspoon ground cinnamon
½ teaspoon ground ginger
½ teaspoon ground nutmeg
½ cup peanuts, roasted and salted
½ cup raisins
½ cup flaked coconut, sweetened
1 medium-sized sweet potato, baked and peeled
2 ripe bananas, peeled
¾ cup brown sugar, firmly packed
⅓ cup vegetable oil
2 teaspoons vanilla extract
2 eggs, slightly beaten

Stir together flour, cinnamon, ginger, nutmeg, peanuts, raisins, and coconut. Set aside.

Add sweet potato and banana flesh to a large bowl. Mash well. Add brown sugar, vegetable oil, vanilla extract, and eggs. Stir together. Add flour mixture and stir only until the dry mixture is wet. Pour into a greased and floured loaf pan. Bake in a 350°F preheated oven for 45 minutes or until toothpick inserted comes out clean. Remove from pan after 10 minutes and cool on a cooling rack.

Sweet Potatoes Are for Vegetarians . . .

Our son and daughter-in-law, Tyler and Jaclyn Garvin, are vegetarians. Actually, Tyler is a vegetarian and his sweet wife accommodates him. They prepared Caribbean Jerk Quinoa and Sweet Potatoes dish to bring over last Thanksgiving. While our family eats lots of vegetables, they're sometimes seasoned with meat products. It's a big help that I can depend on Tyler and Jaclyn to bring a vegetarian dish for family gatherings.

Sweet potatoes add a lot of interest and a whopping dose of nutrition to a vegetarian meal plan. They're a perfect partner for dried beans and lentils. They add a pop of color as well as some added sweetness.

A baked sweet potato is a fine meal all by itself, vegetarian or not. It's filling, tasty, and nutritious. However, a vegetarian has no limit with regards to the many uses of sweet potato. While sweet potatoes are well known as ingredients in desserts, they are just as good in savory dishes, too. While it's not hard to imagine sweet potatoes as a routine component of a vegetarian's diet, its versatility and compatibility might be surprising.

SWEET TIPS

Change up the flavor by substituting your favorite spice blend for Caribbean jerk seasoning.

CARIBBEAN JERK QUINOA AND SWEET POTATO

Yield: 4–6 servings

This vegetarian meal gets a lot of flavor from sautéed vegetables, jerk seasoning, and aromatics. A two-quart slow cooker is large enough when cooking for two. For more servings, use a larger slow cooker, double the recipe, and adjust the cook time.

olive oil
1 large sweet potato, peeled and cut into ½-inch cubes
1 red bell pepper, cut into ½-inch cubes
1 cup butternut squash, cut into ½-inch cubes
1 clove fresh garlic, minced
1 teaspoon onion powder
salt and pepper
3 cups vegetable broth
1 cup quinoa, uncooked
1 teaspoon Caribbean jerk seasoning

Coat a skillet with olive oil. Over medium heat, add sweet potato, bell pepper, butternut squash, garlic, onion powder, and salt and pepper. Sauté for 10 minutes or until vegetables start to soften.

Spray the inside of a 2-quart slow cooker with a nonstick cooking spray. Add sautéed vegetables, vegetable broth, quinoa, and jerk seasoning. Cover and cook on high for 2 hours or until vegetables are tender. Stir before serving.

CHICKEN, POTATO, AND CABBAGE BAKE

Preheat oven to 400°F
Yield: 4 servings

One-pan meals are a spin on one-pot meals. Instead of throwing all the ingredients in a pot, they're arranged on a sheet pan and roasted in the oven. Cover the sheet pan with parchment paper or aluminum foil for easy cleanup. If you like cabbage crisp, cut the wedges thicker. Wedges that are a quarter of an average size head of cabbage will cook soft. Cut potatoes of equal size no more than ¼ inch thick. Save extra salt mixture for another use. I keep it on my work space and season everything from meat to vegetables.

2 tablespoons kosher salt
2 teaspoons ground black pepper
2 teaspoons garlic powder
4 chicken thighs, skin on and bone in
1–2 medium-sized sweet potatoes, peeled and sliced
1–2 medium Yukon gold potatoes, peeled and sliced
cooking oil
1 medium sweet onion, peeled and halved
½ cabbage, cored and cut in 2–4 wedges

Cover large baking pan with parchment paper or aluminum foil and set aside.

Stir together kosher salt, ground black pepper, and garlic powder. Sprinkle salt mixture on both sides of chicken and arrange on baking sheet.

Place potatoes in a medium bowl. Drizzle cooking oil and sprinkle salt mixture over potatoes. Toss to combine. Arrange on baking pan.

Drizzle onion with oil and sprinkle with salt mixture. Place on baking sheet.

Drizzle cabbage wedges with cooking oil and sprinkle with salt mixture. Arrange on baking pan.

Bake in a 400°F preheated oven for 60 minutes or until internal temperature of chicken reaches 165°F.

CHILLED STRAWBERRY SWEET POTATO SOUP

Yield: approximately 1 quart

Don't disregard a cold soup during the winter. The fresh flavors of winter strawberries and navel oranges will brighten a dreary day. They've both been kissed by the sun. If the idea of chilled fruit soup doesn't suit your liking, throw all the ingredients in the food processor, along with a frozen ripe banana, and make smoothies.

1 small sweet potato, baked, cooled, and peeled
16 ounces fresh strawberries, hulled and halved (put a few aside for garnish)
zest of 1 orange (save some zest for garnish)
3 navel oranges
1–2 tablespoons honey
½ cup sour cream or Greek yogurt

Place sweet potato and strawberries in the bowl of a food processor. Place the zest of 1 orange in the food processor. Juice all 3 oranges and add to food processor along with honey. Add sour cream or yogurt and blend until silky smooth.

Chill overnight before serving.

Serve cold. Garnish with leftover strawberries and orange zest. Drizzle with additional honey if needed.

SWEET TIPS

To save time, make the soup ahead and freeze. Wait until ready to serve to make Key Lime Cream.

KEY LIME SWEET POTATO BISQUE WITH KEY LIME CREAM

Yield: 6 servings

As I tried to educate myself on the difference in bisque and soup, I learned that bisque is puréed and thick while soups might be of any consistency. Then I learned that bisque *is from the same root word as* biscuit. *Since I'm all about the biscuit, I dubbed this thick, luscious, puréed soup the bisque that is key lime sweet potato. Key limes are easy to find in Florida grocery stores. They're itty-bitty limes with a sweeter flavor than Persian limes (the ordinary grocery store variety). If key limes aren't available, look for bottled juice or substitute Persian limes (3 key limes is equal to 1 Persian).*

Bisque:

cooking oil
1 sweet onion, peeled and diced
2 carrots, peeled and diced
2 celery stalks, peeled and diced
2–3 cloves of garlic
4 medium-sized sweet potatoes, peeled and cut in chunks
2 Granny Smith apples, peeled, cored, and cut in chunks
2 tablespoons key lime juice
1 quart chicken stock
1 teaspoon ground ginger
¼ teaspoon ground cayenne pepper
salt and pepper, to taste
½ cup half-and-half
key lime zest

Key lime cream:

1 cup heavy whipping cream
1 tablespoon key lime juice
2 tablespoons powdered sugar
1 tablespoon key lime zest plus additional for garnish

Make the bisque

Cover the bottom of a large saucepan with cooking oil. When hot, add onion, carrots, and celery. Cook uncovered for 15 minutes or until soft and the volume is reduced by half. Add garlic and cook 5 additional minutes.

Add remaining ingredients except half-and-half and zest. Cover and simmer for 30 minutes or until sweet potatoes and apples are soft. Purée with an immersion blender. Stir in half-and-half and key lime zest. Taste for seasoning and adjust.

Make the key lime cream

Add cold whipping cream to a medium bowl. Whip with electric mixer until it begins to thicken. Add lime juice, powdered sugar, and 1 tablespoon zest. Whip until stiff peaks form. Add to hot bisque. Garnish with key lime zest.

LENTIL, SWEET POTATO, AND CHIPOTLE PEPPER CHILI

Yield: 8 servings

Even though we eat lots of vegetables, I typically use some form of meat product for seasoning. Having a few vegetarian meals in your recipe collection is smart since vegetarianism is a growing trend. This is a nice version that you can easily convert to vegetarian by using vegetable stock instead of chicken. Control the heat by the amount of chipotle peppers you choose to add. According to my taste buds, one pepper gave it a pleasant kick. I love to cook this in a cast-iron Dutch oven. I chose my enameled one because the acid in tomato products can damage the coating on cast iron that doesn't have an enameled finish. I took this to one of my Bible study classes and shared with my study partners Sheryl Francavilla and Melonie Hall. I didn't have to twist their arms to get them to take home the leftovers. They provided me with wonderful feedback, also. Melonie says, "That recipe was a superfood! I felt better instantly eating it," while Sheryl noted, "That chili was delicious and satisfying."

2 medium sweet onions, peeled and diced
3 carrots, peeled and diced
3 celery stalks, diced
cooking oil
4–5 large cloves garlic, peeled and finely minced
6 ounces tomato paste
16 ounces green lentils, rinsed
28 ounces canned tomatoes, diced
1 quart good-quality chicken stock (or vegetable, for a vegetarian dish)
1–2 chipotle peppers (canned in adobo sauce)
1 medium-sized sweet potato, peeled and diced into 1-inch cubes
1 tablespoon chili powder
salt and pepper, to taste

In a Dutch oven, cook onions, carrots, and celery in a small amount of oil over medium heat for 15 minutes. Add garlic and continue to cook 15 more minutes or until vegetables are tender. Stir occasionally and don't let the vegetables get too brown. Add more cooking oil if needed.

Stir in tomato paste. Add remaining ingredients and stir.

Cover and cook on medium heat for 30 to 45 minutes or until lentils and sweet potatoes are tender. Add additional liquid if needed. Taste for seasoning and adjust. Serve warm.

SPLIT PEA, HAM, AND SWEET POTATO SOUP

Yield: 4–6 servings

My granddaddy would say of this soup, "There ain't a thang in here that can hurt cha." That's how he described dishes he thought were healthy. This soup is made of dried split peas, fresh produce and herbs, lean ham, and homemade stock. It won't "hurt cha" at all. The bonus is that it simmers in the slow cooker while you're free to do something else—or nothing at all if you prefer.

16 ounces dried split peas, rinsed
8 ounces cooked ham, diced
1 large carrot, peeled and diced
2 small or 1 medium-sized sweet potato, peeled and diced
4 cloves garlic, peeled and minced
1 medium sweet onion, diced
2 celery stalks, diced
15 sprigs parsley, large stems removed and leaves roughly chopped
1 tablespoon seasoned salt
1½–2 quarts of chicken or turkey stock, homemade or high-quality commercially prepared

Place dried peas on the bottom of a slow cooker. Add ham. Add vegetables next, ending with parsley on top. Stir seasoned salt into stock and gently pour into slow cooker. Cover and cook on high 4 to 5 hours or low 8 to 10 hours. The longer it sits, the more flavorful it will become. Mash, if desired. Thin with additional stock or water, if needed.

SWEET POTATO AND PEAR SOUP

Yield: 6 servings

A juicy, ripe, and sweet pear is a heavenly delight and rates high on my list of food choices. Sweet potato and pear, plus a balance of savory from onion and chicken stock, is a must-try flavor combination.

1 large sweet onion, peeled and sliced
1 tablespoon cooking oil
4 medium-sized sweet potatoes, peeled and cubed
3 Bartlett pears, cored and sliced (no need to peel)
1 teaspoon ground cinnamon
1 teaspoon kosher salt
½ teaspoon garlic powder
3–4 sprigs fresh thyme
1 quart good-quality chicken stock

Sauté onion in cooking oil until caramelized. Add to slow cooker. Place sweet potatoes and pears in slow cooker.

Add cinnamon, salt, and garlic powder. Tie the sprigs of thyme with kitchen string and place on top. There's no need to put yourself through the laborious task of stripping those tiny leaves from the stem. They will fall off as they cook and you can remove the stems.

Carefully pour chicken stock over slow-cooker contents. Cover and cook on high 3 to 4 hours or low 8 to 10 hours or until sweet potatoes are tender.

Purée with an immersion blender.

SWEET POTATO CAKE DOUGHNUTS WITH VANILLA BUTTERMILK GLAZE

Preheat oil to 350°F
Yield: 36 (2-inch) doughnuts

Fresh made doughnuts are something special, real special. I hear there are companies that exist for the main purpose of providing fresh made doughnuts. These doughnuts are easy to make; it's simply a matter of mixing dry ingredients, mixing wet ingredients, mixing dry and wet together, rolling out dough, and cutting out doughnuts. This recipe makes cake doughnuts as opposed to raised doughnuts that use yeast and require a longer preparation period. Add these to your Christmas breakfast rotation. They're really special.

Doughnuts:

1 medium-sized sweet potato, baked, peeled, and mashed
½ cup buttermilk, full fat
2 eggs
4 tablespoons unsalted butter, melted
1 teaspoon vanilla
3 cups self-rising flour
¾ cup granulated sugar
1 teaspoon ground cinnamon
½ teaspoon ground ginger
½ teaspoon ground nutmeg

Glaze:

2 cups powdered sugar
1 teaspoon vanilla
2–3 tablespoons buttermilk
coconut flakes, sweetened
pecans, chopped

Make doughnuts

Whisk together sweet potato, buttermilk, eggs, butter, and vanilla. Set aside.

Add flour, sugar, cinnamon, ginger, and nutmeg to bowl and stir. Pour sweet potato mixture into dry ingredients and stir with a large wooden spoon or mix with hands.

Turn dough out onto a floured surface. Work with hands until dough holds its shape. Roll or pat out to ½-inch thick. Sprinkle small amount of flour on top of dough and spread evenly.

Cut out rounds with a 2-inch biscuit cutter dipped in flour. Continue with dough scraps until all is used. With the cutout dough still on the hard surface, make a hole in the center by dipping your finger in flour and then pressing down in the dough until a hole is formed.

Working in batches, drop several doughnuts in 2 inches of 350°F cooking oil. Don't overcrowd the pan. Cook for about 1 minute on each side or until brown.

Drain on a cooling rack placed on top of a sheet pan. Cool before glazing.

Make glaze

Mix powdered sugar, vanilla, and 1 tablespoon of buttermilk. Add more buttermilk, a little at the time, until the glaze is smooth and pourable. Dip each doughnut into glaze or drizzle glaze over doughnuts.

While the glaze is still wet on the doughnut, dip the doughnuts in coconut or pecans.

SWEET POTATO CAKE WITH COCONUT CUSTARD FILLING AND BUTTERMILK CINNAMON GLAZE

Preheat oven to 350°F
Yield: 1 (3-layer) cake

Several years ago, I reviewed the cookbook Mary Mac's Tea Room *for the publisher, Andrews McMeel, and stumbled upon their recipe for sweet potato cake. Through that recipe, I was introduced to the notion that you can use grated raw sweet potato as you would use grated carrots. That "aha" moment has served me well and helped me expand my ideas regarding the use of grated raw sweet potato in recipes. I took inspiration from that recipe and created a slightly different version. Give this grand cake a prominent place on your Christmas dessert buffet. You won't be sorry. The old-fashioned boiled custard filling is nostalgic and worth the extra effort.*

Cake:

2½ cups cake flour
1 tablespoon baking powder
½ teaspoon kosher salt
1 tablespoon ground cinnamon
1 medium-sized (about 1½ cups) raw sweet potato, peeled and grated
1 cup pecans, chopped
1½ cups vegetable oil
2 cups granulated sugar
4 large eggs, separated
¼ cup hot water
1 (8-ounce can) crushed pineapple, undrained
1 tablespoon vanilla extract

Filling:

8 tablespoons unsalted butter
¼ teaspoon kosher salt
1 (12-ounce) can evaporated milk
1 cup granulated sugar
3 egg yolks
2 cups coconut flakes, sweetened

Glaze:

¼ cup coconut flakes, sweetened
2 cups powdered sugar
1 teaspoon ground cinnamon
2 tablespoons melted butter, cooled
5 tablespoons buttermilk, approximately

Continued on page 68

Make cake

In a large bowl, sift together cake flour, baking powder, and kosher salt. Stir in ground cinnamon. Add grated sweet potato and pecans. Stir until coated. Set aside.

Add vegetable oil, granulated sugar, egg yolks, and hot water to a large bowl. With an electric mixer, beat until smooth.

Stir in crushed pineapple and the juice along with vanilla extract.

Gradually add flour mixture and stir until the flour disappears.

Beat egg whites to stiff peaks. Fold, don't stir, into batter.

Divide among 3 cake pans that have been greased and floured. Bake in a 350°F preheated oven for 35 minutes or until toothpick inserted into center comes out clean.

Let cakes cool in the pans for 10 minutes. Then, transfer to a cooling rack and allow them to completely cool before icing.

Make filling

Melt butter in a saucepan over low heat. Whisk in kosher salt, evaporated milk, sugar, and egg yolks. Increase the heat to medium and cook for about 10 minutes, whisking frequently, until mixture is of a consistency thicker than gravy.

Whisk in coconut flakes. Remove from heat and let cool before spreading on cake layers.

Make glaze

Add sweetened coconut flakes to a hot skillet. Stir constantly until flakes are toasted and brown. Remove from skillet and set aside.

Whisk together powdered sugar and cinnamon in a medium bowl. Add melted butter and 2 tablespoons of buttermilk. Whisk and add additional buttermilk as needed to create a smooth and pourable glaze.

Assembly:

Place first layer of cake on cake plate. Spread half the coconut custard filling. Repeat with second cake layer and remaining custard filling on top.

Top with third cake layer. Pour glaze over top cake layer. Completely cover top layer and allow some to drip down sides of cake.

Sprinkle toasted coconut on top. Allow glaze to firm up before slicing.

CITRUS GARLIC CORNISH GAME HENS WITH SWEET POTATO CORNBREAD DRESSING

Preheat oven to 375°F
Yield: 4 game hens

Game hens are the perfect entrée for guests: everybody gets their own little chicken. No carving is necessary. They're succulent and flavorful. Marinating in a citrus-based liquid helps tenderize the meat even more and adds flavor, also giving me a chance to take advantage of our backyard citrus grove. When marinating, place the hens in a plastic storage bag and place the storage bag in a baking dish as an insurance against a messy refrigerator in case the bag leaks. Sweet potato cornbread dressing adds a touch of Southern flair to a scrumptious meal. I served this to our friends from Massachusetts, Patti and Bob Keagy, along with zipper peas, lace cornbread, lettuce and tomato salad, and sliced oranges picked from our tree that morning. Dessert was summer berries with sweet potato pone (recipe page 127). They got a heaping dose of Southern food and culture. I think we even heard them say "y'all" once or twice.

4 Cornish game hens, rinsed and placed in a gallon storage bag

Marinade:

½ cup soy sauce
½ cup orange juice, freshly squeezed
½ cup brown sugar
½ cup cooking oil
juice of 1 lemon
4 garlic cloves, peeled and smashed
10–12 fresh sage leaves

Sweet potato cornbread dressing:

6 cups sweet potato cornbread cubes, toasted (recipe page 71)
1 medium sweet onion, diced
2–3 celery stalks, diced
2 tablespoons bacon grease
4–6 cups chicken stock
10–12 fresh sage leaves, finely minced
salt and pepper, to taste

Roasting the hens:

cooking oil
ground black pepper

Continued on page 70

Make marinade

Whisk soy sauce, orange juice, brown sugar, cooking oil, and lemon juice until sugar dissolves. Pour the mixture into the storage bag with the hens. Add garlic and sage. Seal bag and place flat in a baking dish. Marinate for at least 4 hours, but up to 24 hours.

Turn frequently while marinating.

Make dressing

Crumble cornbread cubes into a large bowl. Set aside.

Sauté onion and celery in bacon grease over medium-low heat until soft. Add to bowl with bread cubes. Stir in enough chicken stock to wet the bread cubes. Add sage, salt, and pepper. Stir.

Make hens

Remove the hens from the marinade and wipe dry. Fill cavities with cornbread stuffing. If there's more than needed to stuff the cavities, bake the additional dressing separately. Brush the outside of the hen with cooking oil. Sprinkle lightly with pepper. Place breast-side up on a rack in a roasting pan. Secure the legs with kitchen twine or close the cavity with toothpicks.

Bake at 350°F for 1 hour or until the internal temperature of the hens reaches 165°F.

SWEET POTATO CORNBREAD

Preheat oven to 350°F
Yield: 1 (9-inch) round

The notion of sugar in cornbread is enough to send some Southerners on a rant and rampage. It's one of those things that evoke strong feelings for some reason. Ordinarily, I don't add sugar to my cornbread, but I don't think the world is coming to an end if I hear that my neighbor does. I added a tiny bit of sugar to this recipe to contrast the saltiness of bacon and cheese, the tang of buttermilk, and to amplify the natural sweetness of sweet potato. So, the reasons are purely culinary and have nothing to do with tradition. I trust my membership into the Genuine Southerners' Club is still intact.

This cornbread is a great pal of soups and stews. It goes well with most any flavor profile and spice level.

4 strips of uncooked bacon
1 medium-sized sweet potato, baked and skin removed
2 cups buttermilk
4 large eggs
2 cups self-rising flour
2 cups medium or coarse ground cornmeal
¼ cup granulated sugar
1 cup sharp cheddar cheese, grated

Fry bacon crispy in a 9-inch cast-iron skillet. Remove bacon, crumble, and set aside. Don't dare think about discarding the bacon drippings, but remove the skillet from the heat so they don't burn up. We will get back to them shortly.

Place sweet potato flesh in medium bowl and mash. Add buttermilk and eggs. Whisk until mixed well. Set aside.

Measure flour, cornmeal, and sugar into a large mixing bowl. Add crumbled bacon and cheddar cheese. Stir until bacon and cheese are coated with cornmeal mixture.

Add wet ingredients to cornmeal mixture and stir well. If mixture is too thick to be pourable, add a tad bit more buttermilk as needed. It should be thick but pourable.

Reheat skillet with bacon drippings (that you didn't discard) until it begins to smoke. Drop a tiny amount of the batter into the skillet. If it sizzles, the skillet is hot enough.

Pour batter into hot skillet. Bake in a 350°F preheated oven for 45 minutes or until the top has browned to your liking.

SWEET POTATO POUND CAKE WITH MEYER LEMON GLAZE

Preheat oven to 325°F
Yield: 1 cake

If I was limited to only one dessert for the rest of my being, it would be pound cake. The simplicity of flavor for this gold standard Southern dessert is comforting and familiar. The cake is so named because the original ingredients consisted of a pound each of flour, sugar, butter, and eggs. The texture is meant to be dense yet moist. It has a pleasant silky mouth feel. Honestly, everything about pound cake is glorious. Sweet potato pound cake is denser than a plain pound cake but retains the hallmark moist texture. I added cream cheese for more structure to support the weight of sweet potato flesh. Our Meyer lemon tree offered up ripe lemons at the time I baked this cake. I was happy to add them to the glaze, and their flavor complemented the warm spices and sweetness of the sweet potato. This cake is grand enough for a Christmas dessert buffet table.

Cake:

1½ cups unsalted butter, room temperature
8 ounces cream cheese, room temperature
2 cups sugar
2 cups sweet potato, baked, peeled, and mashed (approximately 2 medium-sized sweet potatoes)
6 eggs, room temperature
3 cups cake flour
2 teaspoons baking powder
¼ teaspoon salt
1 teaspoon ground cinnamon
¼ teaspoon ground nutmeg
¼ teaspoon ground ginger
1 teaspoon vanilla extract

Glaze:

4 tablespoons melted butter
2 cups powdered sugar
2–3 tablespoons Meyer lemon juice
zest from 1 Meyer lemon

Make cake

Grease and flour a tube pan or Bundt pan. In a stand mixer, mix butter and cream cheese. Add sugar and sweet potato. Cream on medium speed for about 5 minutes until light and fluffy. With mixer on low, add eggs one a time and mix well after each addition.

In a small bowl, mix together flour, baking powder, salt, cinnamon, nutmeg, and ginger. Slowly add flour mixture to larger bowl and mix after each addition. Remove bowl from mixer and stir in vanilla extract. Pour batter into a prepared pan. Bake in a 325°F preheated oven for 70 minutes or until knife inserted comes out clean. Remove from oven and let cool in pan for 15 minutes. After 15 minutes, gently loosen cake and transfer to a wire rack. Let cool completely before glazing.

Make glaze

Stir together melted butter and powdered sugar. Slowly add lemon juice until desired consistency is obtained. Glaze should be thick yet pourable. Garnish top of cake with lemon zest while the glaze is still wet.

Chapter 3

SPRING

Renew and refresh are verbs associated with spring. Flowering plants burst forth with new colorful blooms that willingly release their natural fragrance. Trees, barren for months, show signs of new growth. The weather is pleasant, for the most part. Skies are so blue and bright they almost hurt your eyes. Grass, brown from cold weather and freezing temperatures, turn a beautiful shade of Easter grass green. Birds happily chirp along as they forage and build nests. Folks are brave enough to venture outdoors wearing shorts that show off snow-white legs that haven't seen sun for months. Spring is a season that plays pleasantly on our senses and overall feelings of well-being. Spring is a beautiful season filled with many opportunities for celebrations such as Easter, Passover, Mother's Day, and graduations.

I learned the religious significance of Easter early in life; in fact, I don't recall not knowing it. My grandparents, devout in their Christian faith, helped us cut our teeth on Bible stories. Celebration of the secular part of major holidays was accepted but the real meaning of the holiday, the part that had religious significance, was boldly stressed. I appreciate the teaching I received and the foundation it formed for my faith walk.

I associate the secular side of Easter with dotted Swiss fabric. My mother was obsessed with that fabric for Easter dresses. She would choose fabric and patterns with help from my grandmother, an excellent seamstress, who made the dresses for us. My two sisters and I asked for pink dotted Swiss fabric. My mother recoiled at that suggestion, saying pink isn't a good choice, blaming my hair color. According to her estimation, redheads couldn't wear pink. Apparently, that was a hard and fast fashion rule that she was loath to violate. In fact, she was loath to get anywhere close to violating the rule. My hair wasn't red but auburn. As an adult, she complimented me often when I wore pink. My hair remained auburn but I suppose the rule had relaxed enough that she found auburn-haired people in pink tolerable. Today, shades of pink are top clothing choices for me. However, I still haven't had a pink dotted Swiss Easter dress.

When my kids were little, Mother's Day was a favorite holiday. I took full advantage of my day and made the day exactly what I wanted it to be. I chose not to cook at all that day. We would attend church services together and afterwards we participated in an activity of my choice. For many years, we would go canoeing. As the children got older, they became less enjoyable on a canoe trip. Complaints of "I'm bored" and "My back hurts" and "I'm hot" and "Why does this have to take so long" took away my joy of canoeing. So, I had to come up with other plans. One year, I had them help plant a rose garden. Another year, I asked my teenaged daughters to cook a traditional Southern meal for me. The meal was delicious and I was so proud. In the process of meal preparation, they used every pot, pan, frying pan, and cooking implement I had in the kitchen. Flour was strewn from stem to stern. The kitchen was finally cleaned properly years later when it was demolished for renovation. Memories of Mother's Day with my young children are treasured and sacred.

I made sure to always recognize my mother on Mother's Day. As an adult, I never lived in the same town as she so I rarely saw her on the actual day of the holiday. Frequently, I sent her flowers. Without exception, I called her to wish her a happy Mother's Day. After my mother died March 2009, I expected holidays to be sad for years following her death. I knew the day of her birthday would cause me sadness. What I didn't anticipate was the overwhelming grief that consumed my soul the first Mother's Day, May 2009, I didn't have a mother. It was the kind of grief that takes your breath away and makes you feel that you won't be able to carry on. It's the kind of grief that overpowers everything that was once joyful and wipes it from your memory. It's the kind of grief that rips away your personality and reduces you to a quivering, pitiful mess with no purpose. It's the kind of grief that makes you fearful your heart might explode. What I knew for sure is that I could not bear to repeat that horrible grief again. So, the next year, we filled up our backyard with family, friends, food, and a jazz band to celebrate Mother's Day. It was a wonderful event and a fitting way to honor my mother. She loved music, food, and fun gatherings. She would have been especially proud that her grandson, my only son, was the bass player in the jazz band. I still miss my mother as I'm sure I always will. Time has eased some of the pain but I long for the day that Mother's Day 2009 is but a faint memory.

SPRING RECIPES

Apple and Sweet Potato Braids
78
Sweet Potato and Bacon Hash with Baked Eggs
81
Baked Sweet Potatoes with Rum Raisin Sauce
82
Belle's Sweet Potato Chewies
85
Oatmeal Sweet Potato Cookies
87
Pulled Pork Tacos with Spicy Sweet Potato Slaw
88
Roasted Sweet and Yukon Gold Potatoes
91
Rosemary Sweet Potato Flatbread
92
Sweet Potato Chocolate Chip Cookies
95
Sweet Potato Coconut Fritters
96
Sweet Potato Skillet Cake with Broiled Coconut and Pecan Icing
99
Asparagus, Sweet Potato, and Leek Pie
101
Overnight Sweet Potato Belgian Waffles
102
Roasted Sweet Potato, Asparagus, and Sweet Pea Pasta Salad
106
Strawberry Sweet Potato Bread with Glaze
109

APPLE AND SWEET POTATO BRAIDS

Preheat oven to 350°F
Yield: 4 braids

May is the month of graduation parties. If brunch is in your plans, these pastries deserve a spot on the buffet. A filling of sweet potatoes, Meyer lemon juice, cream cheese, and maple syrup welcome a layer of cooked Granny Smith apples. Premade puff pastry shells lighten the workload. If another variety of lemon is substituted for Meyer lemon, the amounts may need adjusting. The amount of sweetening might need adjusting since Meyer lemons aren't as tart as ordinary lemons.

Pastry:

2 (17.3-ounce) boxes of puff pastry shells. Thaw according to package directions. Roll to approximately ¼ inch thick when ready to use.

Apple filling:

4 tablespoons unsalted butter
¼ cup brown sugar, firmly packed
1 teaspoon ground cinnamon
3 Granny Smith apples, peeled, cored, and cut in 1-inch cubes

Sweet potato filling:

1 medium-sized sweet potato, baked, peeled, and cooled
8 ounces cream cheese, softened
4 tablespoons maple syrup
4 tablespoons Meyer lemon juice

Topping:

1 large egg
1 tablespoon of water
raw sugar

Make apple filling

Add butter, brown sugar, and cinnamon to a skillet. When melted, stir in apples and cook until tender. Set aside to cool.

Make sweet potato filling

Add all ingredients to large bowl and beat with an electric mixer until smooth. Arrange both thawed pastry sheets lengthwise on parchment-lined baking sheets. On the outer third of both sides of the pastry sheet, cut an equal number of diagonal strips the length of the pastry.

Divide the sweet potato filling between the pastry sheets and place it down the middle third, spreading evenly. Divide the apple filling between the pastry sheets, placing it atop the sweet potato filling.

Bring the end of the pastry sheet up toward the middle. Take the strips alternatively from each side and wrap across the top of the pastry sheet.

Make topping

Whisk 1 egg and 1 tablespoon of water. Brush tops of pastry. Sprinkle tops with raw sugar.

Bake at 350°F for 30 minutes or until golden brown.

Remove from oven and let cool before slicing.

SWEET TIPS

For a spicy version, substitute your favorite sausage for bacon.

SWEET POTATO AND BACON HASH WITH BAKED EGGS

Preheat oven to 350°F
Yield: 2–4

In recent years, folks have gone hash crazy. Modern hash doesn't resemble the canned corned beef hash I grew up with. Many types of vegetables and proteins are used to create different varieties of hash. So, hash is a super star. Make a hash from a super star ingredient, like sweet potatoes, and you've got something fittin' to eat. Every brunch should have hash. The vegetable portion can be made ahead and refrigerated. When it's time to serve, put it in the skillet to reheat before baking the eggs.

4–6 strips of uncooked bacon, diced
2 medium-sized raw sweet potatoes, peeled or unpeeled, in 1-inch dice
3–4 green onions, sliced
1 tablespoon fresh rosemary, finely minced
kosher salt and pepper, to taste
4 fresh eggs

Over medium heat, cook diced bacon in a 9-inch cast-iron skillet. Cook bacon until fat is rendered and the bacon gets crispy.

Throw sweet potatoes, onions (include the greens! I don't know why those aren't used), and rosemary in the skillet on top of the bacon and its grease. Stir to make sure everything is coated in bacon grease. Press out into a single layer. Sprinkle with kosher salt and pepper. Continue to cook over medium heat. Check the bottom side of the sweet potatoes and stir them when they start to brown. Stir occasionally until the potatoes are tender but not mushy.

Make four little round wells in the hash for the eggs. Crack an egg into each well and bake at 350°F for 10 minutes or until the white is set.

Serve immediately. (Well, take it out of the oven first, and then serve immediately.)

NOTE

If you're cooking hash for a group and the number of guests exceeds the capacity of your largest skillet, transfer the hash to a large baking sheet as it's done. Once the baking sheet is filled, make as many wells in the hash as you want for eggs. Bake eggs and hash on the baking sheet.

BAKED SWEET POTATOES WITH RUM RAISIN SAUCE

Preheat oven to 350°F
Yield: 4 servings

Serve this for Easter dinner alongside your baked ham. The rum raisin sauce turns a baked sweet potato into an event. Warning: the gussied-up sweet potato might steal the show from the Easter ham.

2 tablespoons dark raisins
2 tablespoons rum, spiced or regular
¼ cup unsalted butter
¼ cup brown sugar, firmly packed
4 medium-sized sweet potatoes, baked

Add raisins and rum to a small bowl and set aside for at least 30 minutes to allow the raisins to plump.

To a small saucepan, add butter and brown sugar over medium-low heat. Stir until mixture melts and begins to bubble.

Remove from heat. This is an important step to keep you from burning down your kitchen as you add rum, which is highly flammable. *Remove from heat*. I just said it again.

Add rum and raisin mixture to butter and sugar. Mix well.

Serve hot over baked sweet potatoes.

SWEET TIPS

For a different flavor profile, substitute dried cranberries for raisins.

Sweet Potatoes Are for Dogs . . .

I am a basset hound person. I unashamedly admit it, claim it, and live it. Their exaggerated features give them the look of a living and breathing cartoon. Throw in their sweet, docile disposition, and you've got a wonderful creature that captures my heart and attention.

Our current, and second, basset hound is Belle, a six-year-old female. Belle came into our family as a puppy shortly after losing our first basset, Sadie, who died just before turning twelve.

Basset hounds have a tendency to gain weight easily; largely because they have no self-control when confronted with anything they consider food. Extra weight poses health concerns for them. We regulate Belle's food and only give her vegetables as treats. Of course, anything she finds on the counter is fair game as far as she's concerned. Bassets are surprisingly tall when they stand on their hind legs to counter surf. If you have a basset hound around and leave out food that you want to keep, it has to be placed on a high counter. As my grandmother would say, "We have to put it up in the top of the house."

In addition to bits of raw carrots and green bean snaps, Belle loves pieces of raw sweet potato. She plows through small pieces of vegetables in a heartbeat. Sweet potato chewies last a little longer for her and keep her occupied as she chews, plus she gets the added benefit of sweet potato nutrients.

Sweet potato chewies are suitable for any season, anytime. Freeze a batch so you'll always have some available.

BELLE'S SWEET POTATO CHEWIES

Preheat oven to 250°F
Yield: 6–8 pieces

Dogs love sweet potatoes, too. Oven-dried sweet potatoes are chewy and give them a longer lasting treat. Make a batch and keep them in the freezer. I like to remove the sweet potatoes from the oven while the center is a little soft and pliable. Be sure to cut the sweet potato at least ¼ inch thick. They shrink up considerably when dried.

Slice a medium or large sweet potato lengthwise into ¼-inch-thick slabs. Place on a parchment paper–covered large baking sheet. Bake at 250°F for 8 to 10 hours or until dried.

SWEET TIPS

For a touch of citrus, substitute orange extract for half of the vanilla extract.

OATMEAL SWEET POTATO COOKIES

Preheat oven to 350°F
Yield: approximately 6 dozen (2-inch) cookies

My husband loves chewy oatmeal raisin cookies. The trick to soft, chewy cookies is to include brown sugar and chill the dough before baking. The molasses in brown sugar adds moisture. Chilled dough doesn't spread when baked like room temperature dough, which results in thin, crispy cookies. I combined elements from soft, chewy oatmeal cookies with spices from carrot cake, one of his favorite cakes, to come up with these cookies, which have the cookie texture and the cake flavors that he loves.

2 cups self-rising flour
1½ teaspoons ground cinnamon
1½ teaspoon ground nutmeg
1 cup unsalted butter, softened
½ cup granulated sugar
1½ cup brown sugar, firmly packed
2 large eggs
1 tablespoon vanilla extract
3 cups quick-cooking oatmeal
1½ cup raisins
1 medium-sized sweet potato, peeled and grated (about 2 cups)

Stir together flour, cinnamon, and nutmeg. Set aside.

Cream butter, sugars, eggs, and vanilla until smooth.

Stir flour mixture into wet ingredients and mix with a large spoon until the dough is wet. Stir in oatmeal, raisins, and grated sweet potato until well mixed. Cover bowl and chill for at least 2 hours.

Shape heaping tablespoons of dough into balls. Place 2 inches apart on a cookie sheet lined with parchment, a baking mat, or sprayed with a nonstick cooking spray.

Bake at 350°F for 12 minutes or until the bottoms have begun to brown and tops are no longer glossy.

Let sit on cooking sheet for 2 minutes. Remove to a cooling rack and completely cool.

PULLED PORK TACOS WITH SPICY SWEET POTATO SLAW

Yield: 2 cups of slaw

Raw sweet potato will make you forget about using carrots in coleslaw. They're not starchy like raw potatoes so they're mighty fine in this recipe. Napa cabbage is a little bitter so I made a slightly sweet dressing for the slaw. The mayonnaise I use doesn't contain sugar. If another brand is used, the amount of sugar in the dressing might need to be adjusted. Let the slaw marinate for at least an hour for the best flavor. In addition to a taco topping, it's a great side dish to use for any occasion where you'd normally serve coleslaw. This makes a wonderful, quick meal for families that find themselves running in different directions but want to have a family meal when possible. Use leftover pulled pork and make the slaw ahead of time. Dinner is ready as soon as the pork and tacos are heated, so you've got time for a great meal and still be able to get everyone where they need to go.

Spicy sweet potato slaw:

2 cups raw sweet potato, peeled and grated
2 cups Napa cabbage, shredded
2 green onions, thinly sliced

Dressing:

⅓ cup mayonnaise (I used Duke's brand)
1 tablespoon sugar
1 tablespoon apple cider vinegar
1 tablespoon pickled jalapeños, finely diced (more or less to taste)
½ teaspoon ground black pepper
½ teaspoon kosher salt

Pork tacos:

pulled pork
soft taco shells, flour or corn
spicy sweet potato slaw (recipe below)

Make slaw and dressing

Mix all ingredients and set aside. Pour dressing over slaw and stir well. Refrigerate until ready for use.

Assemble tacos

To heat tacos, follow the directions on the package. Place a spoonful of pulled pork on each warm taco shell followed by a spoonful of slaw. The slaw is so creamy I didn't add an additional sauce for the taco. Three elements are all that's needed for this quick meal.

SWEET TIPS

To save time, substitute packaged shredded slaw mix for Napa cabbage.

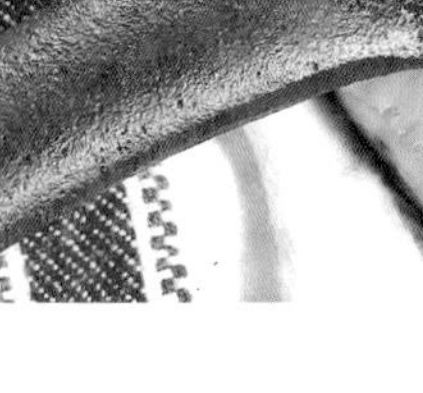

SWEET TIPS

For added color, substitute any color potato for Yukon gold.

ROASTED SWEET AND YUKON GOLD POTATOES

Preheat oven to 400°F
Yield: 4 servings

Rosemary's woodsy flavor is a nice friend to white and sweet earthy potatoes. The potatoes crisp up on the outside but stay soft and creamy on the inside. Skins on or skins off is a matter of preference. I leave them on. They're good served hot from the oven or at room temperature. For a picnic, let them cool completely before packaging in an air tight container. They're a nice change of pace from bagged chips and will be a welcome accompaniment to fried chicken or sandwiches.

1 medium-sized sweet potato, washed and cut into 1-inch cubes
2 medium/small Yukon gold potatoes, washed and cut into 1-inch cubes
olive oil
1 teaspoon kosher salt
¼ teaspoon ground black pepper
¼ teaspoon garlic powder
3 tablespoons fresh rosemary, minced and divided

Cover a large baking sheet with aluminum foil and spray with a nonstick cooking spray.

Place potatoes on baking sheet. Drizzle with olive oil. Add kosher salt, pepper, garlic powder, and two tablespoons of minced rosemary. Toss to coat well. Arrange in a single layer.

Roast in a 400°F preheated oven for 30 minutes. Flip the potatoes over and roast for an additional 30 minutes or until they are well browned. Remove from oven and sprinkle with additional rosemary before serving.

ROSEMARY SWEET POTATO FLATBREAD

Preheat oven to 450°F
Yield: 1 (11 x 17) sheet pan

If you typically serve lamb for Easter, this is your bread. You might be unaware that you're searching for it, yet it appears before your very eyes. The orange hue of the dough and the detail of fresh rosemary, coarse salt, and fresh cracked black pepper on the surface give the bread a visual appeal. The flavors complement lamb or any meat seasoned with rosemary. Dough spread thin over the entire surface of the large baking sheet will result in crispy crackers. For soft bread, spread the dough thicker in a smaller baking sheet. Tear apart and serve.

2 cups self-rising flour
2 tablespoons fresh rosemary, chopped and divided
1 small sweet potato, baked
⅓ cup vegetable oil
½ cup water
olive oil
coarse salt
fresh cracked black pepper

Add flour and 1 tablespoon rosemary to a bowl and gently stir together with your fingers.

In a separate bowl, add sweet potato, vegetable oil, and water. Mash sweet potato with a fork and stir until well blended.

Add wet mixture to dry. Stir with a wooden spoon just until dough is wet.

Turn out onto a lightly floured surface. Sprinkle dough with additional flour. Gently work the flour into the dough, add more as needed until the dough is no longer sticky and holds its shape.

Press the dough onto a parchment-paper–lined 11 x 17 sheet pan. Make several pricks with a fork on the top of the dough.

Brush with olive oil. Sprinkle on the remaining rosemary, coarse salt, and fresh ground black pepper.

Bake in a 450°F oven for 15 minutes or until the top starts to brown.

SWEET POTATO CHOCOLATE CHIP COOKIES

Preheat oven to 350°F
Yield: approximately 3½ dozen (3-inch) cookies

You will be pleasantly surprised by how nicely sweet potato plays with chocolate chips in this spin on a traditional and popular cookie: chocolate chip. The flavor combination is outstanding. The cookie is soft and somewhat poofy, not like a traditional chocolate chip cookie that's usually crunchy. Consider this unexpected cookie for an end of the year gift for teachers. It's almost guaranteed the teacher will never forget you or your child.

2 cups self-rising flour
1 teaspoon ground cinnamon
1 cup milk chocolate chips
1 medium-sized sweet potato, baked, cooled, and peeled
1 cup unsalted butter, softened
2 eggs, slightly beaten
¾ cup granulated sugar
¾ cup brown sugar, firmly packed
1 teaspoon vanilla extract
½ teaspoon lemon extract

Add flour and cinnamon to a medium bowl. Stir to mix. Add chocolate chips and stir until combined. Set aside.

Add sweet potato, butter, eggs, granulated sugar, brown sugar, and extracts to a large bowl. Cream with an electric mixer.

Gradually add the flour mixture to the wet mixture, stirring only until all the flour has disappeared.

Drop teaspoons of dough onto a large baking sheet lined with parchment paper or a baking mat, spacing the dough 2 inches apart.

Bake in a 350°F preheated oven for 17 minutes or until the edges begin to brown.

Cool on a cooling rack.

SWEET POTATO COCONUT FRITTERS

Yield: approximately 36 fritters

Give any self-respecting Southerner a little bit of fruit or vegetable and we can fry up a fritter. A fritter is nothing more than deep-fried dough enhanced with fruit or vegetables. Traditionally, fritters were a way to use up leftovers. You've got to give fritters credit for a name that's fun to say, too. Let sweet potato coconut fritters be an unexpected surprise next to your Easter ham.

2½ cups self-rising flour
½ cup granulated sugar
1 tablespoon ground cinnamon
½ teaspoon ground nutmeg
½ teaspoon ground ginger
1 medium-sized sweet potato, baked, cooled, and peeled
2 large eggs
¾ cup buttermilk
2 tablespoons vegetable oil
1 tablespoon vanilla extract
1 cup coconut flakes, sweetened
cooking oil for frying
powdered sugar for dusting

Add flour, sugar, cinnamon, nutmeg, and ginger to a bowl. Whisk lightly.

In another bowl, add sweet potato, eggs, buttermilk, vegetable oil, vanilla extract, and coconut. Mash the potato and combine the ingredients.

Mix wet and dry ingredients together.

Pour cooking oil into a pan to a depth of at least 1 inch and heat to 350°F. When the oil reaches the correct temperature, drop teaspoons of dough into the hot oil. I use one teaspoon to scoop up the dough and another teaspoon to push the dough into the hot grease. Work in batches and don't crowd the pan.

Fry 1 to 2 minutes or until medium brown on one side. Flip and repeat on the other side. Remove with a slotted spoon to a cooling rack. Continue with remaining dough.

Dust with powdered sugar.

SWEET TIPS

Serve each piece with a dollop of fresh sweetened whipped cream sprinkled with toasted coconut.

SWEET POTATO SKILLET CAKE WITH BROILED COCONUT AND PECAN ICING

Preheat oven to 350°F
Yield: 1 (9-inch) round cake

Everybody needs a skillet cake recipe, of some description, in their recipe files. They come together quickly and make just enough cake to soothe everyone's sweet tooth, but don't leave you with tons of leftover cake. Not that there's anything wrong with leftover cake, but sometimes the temptation of half a layer cake staring at you is simply too much to overcome. You can rest assured this cake won't live to see the light of the next day. This cake has an old-fashioned broiled icing, which we seem to have largely forgotten. They've given way to fluffy cream cheese or whipped cream icings.

Cake:

2 extra large eggs
1 cup granulated sugar
½ cup buttermilk
½ teaspoon baking soda
2 tablespoons unsalted butter, melted and cooled
1 medium-sized sweet potato, baked and flesh removed and mashed
1 cup self-rising flour
1 teaspoon ground cinnamon
¼ teaspoon ground ginger

Icing:

¼ cup unsalted butter
⅔ cup brown sugar, firmly packed
3 tablespoons buttermilk
pinch of kosher salt
1 cup coconut flakes, sweetened

Make cake

Beat together eggs and sugar until creamy and pale yellow. In the same bowl, add buttermilk, baking soda, melted butter, and mashed sweet potato. Stir until mixed.

Continued on page 100

Add flour, cinnamon, and ginger to a small bowl and stir lightly.

Add flour mixture to wet ingredients and stir with a large wooden spoon until mixed.

Pour into a well-seasoned 9-inch cast-iron skillet. You may substitute a greased and floured 8-inch square pan.

Bake at 350°F for 30 minutes or until toothpick inserted comes out clean.

Remove from oven and prepare icing.

Make icing

Cook butter, brown sugar, buttermilk, and salt in a small pan over medium heat, stirring constantly, until the butter and sugar have melted. Add coconut and continue stirring until the mixture reaches a medium rolling boil.

Immediately, pour icing on top of warm skillet cake and spread across the entire surface of the cake.

Place under a broiler for 2 to 3 minutes or until browned. *Do not get distracted.* Once the topping starts to brown, you've got but a few seconds that separates browned from burned.

Remove from oven and completely cool on a cooling rack before cutting.

ASPARAGUS, SWEET POTATO, AND LEEK PIE

Preheat oven to 400°F

Yield: 1 (9-inch) pie

I've never grown asparagus and I don't think I'm cut out for it—I'm in the "plant it and eat it in the same year" camp. I violated that rule by growing pineapple that requires about two years before harvest. One violation is more than enough for me. Two is more than I can handle. Plus, pineapple is suited to the climate in the Deep South. Asparagus would suffer in my garden, but I'm always happy to see it in the grocery stores. This pie deserves a spot on your Easter or Mother's Day buffet. Leeks are grown in sand and take special care to clean well.

1 medium leek, cut crosswise, whites only
1 medium-sized sweet potato, peeled and diced
olive oil
salt and pepper
½–¾ lb. thin asparagus, tough ends trimmed
1 (9-inch) prepared pie crust
½ lb. Gruyère cheese, grated
4 large eggs
1½ cups half-and-half
½ teaspoon kosher salt
½ teaspoon ground black pepper

Place sliced leeks in ice water and let them sit for 10 to 15 minutes. Carefully remove so as to not disturb the debris in the bottom of the bowl. Drain. Sauté the leeks in olive oil over medium heat until tender and slightly caramelized. Remove from heat and let cool.

Place diced sweet potatoes in a single layer on a large baking sheet lined with parchment paper (leave half the sheet empty for the asparagus). Drizzle olive oil over sweet potatoes and sprinkle with salt and pepper. Toss to coat.

Roast in a 400°F preheated oven for 20 minutes.

Add asparagus to the same sheet pan as the sweet potatoes. Drizzle with olive oil and sprinkle salt and pepper. Roast for an additional 10 minutes. Remove from oven and set aside. Reduce oven heat to 350°F.

Spread grated cheese evenly in the bottom of the pie crust. Add leeks. Top with sweet potatoes and asparagus.

In a large bowl, whisk eggs, half-and-half, kosher salt, and pepper. Pour in pie shell. Place pie on a baking sheet to catch drips and spills and place in oven. Bake for 50 minutes or until center is set. Let sit for 10 minutes before cutting.

OVERNIGHT SWEET POTATO BELGIAN WAFFLES

Yield: 6 (6-inch) Belgian waffles

I stumbled (gracefully, of course) upon this recipe in the material that came with my Waring Pro Professional Belgian Waffle Maker. It's become a favorite breakfast item for overnight house guests. The night before, you mix most of the ingredients and leave it out on the counter. If you're worried about food safety, all I can say is I've made this recipe more times than I can count and it's been perfectly safe. In the morning, a few fresh items are added and then everyone gets to make their own hot waffle whenever they're ready. I set up a waffle bar with different toppings such as apple, cherry, and blueberry pie filling, fresh whipped cream, toasted pecans, and a variety of syrups and flavored butters. I've adapted this recipe to suit my taste and preference for certain ingredients. Sweet potato purée adds flavor and nutrition. For regular buttermilk waffles, omit sweet potato and cinnamon and increase buttermilk to 2 cups.

½ cup water (105°F)
1 tablespoon granulated sugar
1 packet active dry yeast (2¼ teaspoons)
1½ cups buttermilk (105°F)
½ cup unsalted butter, melted and cooled
1 teaspoon kosher salt
2 cups all-purpose flour
2 large eggs, slightly beaten
1 tablespoon vanilla extract
¼ teaspoon baking soda
1 medium-sized sweet potato, baked, cooled, and peeled
1 teaspoon ground cinnamon

Mix water, sugar, and active yeast and let stand for 10 minutes or until foamy. If it doesn't foam, your yeast is dead and you'll need to throw that out and start over. Whisk in buttermilk, melted butter, and salt. Whisk in flour until smooth.

Wrap bowl tightly with plastic wrap and leave on the counter overnight. Be sure to allow lots of room for expansion in the bowl. The batter will at least double in size. I learned that lesson the hard way and came into my kitchen the next morning to find waffle batter dripping from my kitchen counter.

In the morning, add eggs, vanilla extract, baking soda, sweet potato, and ground cinnamon to a small bowl. Whisk until smooth. Add sweet potato mixture to flour mixture and whisk just until well incorporated.

Prepare waffles on waffle maker according to manufacturer's recommendations. Serve warm.

For batches, keep waffles warm by placing them on a baking sheet in a 200°F oven. They're best freshly made and eaten straight from the waffle maker. If folks are lined up at your waffle maker and complaining they might perish waiting on their turn, give them a piece of fruit to tide them over. Only use the batch method in case of emergencies. I'm not sure what constitutes a waffle emergency. That's for you to decide.

Sweet Potatoes Are for Caterers . . .

When Peggy Davenport's career in Corporate America ended, she sought a job that would allow her to work at home. Before long, she made a logical connection: she loves to cook and many of her friends found it hard to prepare a home-cooked meal. She started selling fully prepared, made-from-scratch meals to her friends and neighbors. Her primary methods of advertising were word of mouth and Facebook postings. Soon, her business grew to the point that she needed to name it. Davenport Daily Delights became a popular go-to for folks who wanted to include family meals into their hectic schedules.

She soon added catering to her service offerings. I'm mighty glad she did, because she catered two events for me last year: my book signing for *Biscuits: Sweet and Savory Southern Recipes for the All-American Kitchen* and my son's wedding reception. Along with providing excellent food at a competitive price, Peggy is a delight. Her winning personality makes her as fun as her food is good.

For her catering events, Peggy needs fresh, wholesome ingredients that are economical, available, versatile, and hold up well once they're cooked. Sweet potatoes fit the bill. She uses them frequently and they're included in some of her most popular dishes, such as Sweet Potato and Black Bean Burritos and Spinach Quesadillas with Three Pepper and Sweet Potato Salsa.

ROASTED SWEET POTATO, ASPARAGUS, AND SWEET PEA PASTA SALAD

Preheat oven to 400°F
Yield: 8 (1½ cups) servings

This pasta salad is loaded with vegetables. Asparagus and sweet peas are spring favorites. Lemon vinaigrette adds an additional burst of flavor. For make ahead, roast the vegetables and make the dressing. Store them separately in the refrigerator. When ready to use, reheat the vegetables and cook the pasta. Mix them together and add dressing while warm. This recipe is easily doubled for large gatherings. It's portable so it can be made at home and transported if necessary.

Pasta:

4 cups sweet potatoes, peeled and cut into 1-inch dicc
1 bunch asparagus, trimmed and cut into 1-inch pieces
2 cups frozen sweet peas, thawed
1 red bell pepper, 1-inch dice
1 yellow bell pepper, 1-inch dice
½ cup olive oil
salt and pepper, to taste
1 lb. whole wheat penne pasta
1 cup crumbled goat cheese

Lemon vinaigrette:

¾ cup extra virgin olive oil
¾ cup fresh lemon juice
zest of 1 lemon
¼ cup sugar
1 teaspoon salt
1 teaspoon ground black pepper

Make pasta

Place sweet potatoes, asparagus, sweet peas, and other diced vegetables in a single layer on a large baking sheet covered with parchment paper. Add olive oil, salt, and pepper. Toss to coat. Roast at 400°F for 20 minutes or until tender.

Boil pasta to al dente according to package directions. Drain. While the vegetables are still warm, toss with pasta, goat cheese, and lemon vinaigrette.

Make vinaigrette

Mix all ingredients together and pour over pasta salad.

STRAWBERRY SWEET POTATO BREAD WITH GLAZE

Preheat oven to 350°F
Yield: 1 loaf

Quick breads are good any time of the year. This bread is beautiful with the golden hue from sweet potatoes and the ruby red strawberries. Strawberries have high water content and will melt into the batter if they're diced. They show up as a red blotch instead of cut strawberries. I slice the strawberries instead of dice so you can identify them inside the bread.

Bread:

½ cup unsalted butter, room temperature
1½ cups granulated sugar
2 large eggs
1 medium-sized sweet potato, baked, cooled, and peeled
1 tablespoon vanilla extract
2 cups self-rising flour
1 teaspoon ground cinnamon
½ teaspoon ground nutmeg
½ teaspoon ground cloves
½ teaspoon ground ginger
2 cups fresh strawberries, hulled and sliced

Glaze:

2 tablespoons strawberry jam
2 tablespoons butter
2 cups powdered sugar
1 tablespoon lime or lemon juice
milk, optional

Make bread

Place butter, sugar, eggs, sweet potato, and vanilla extract in a bowl. Beat with an electric mixer on low speed until all ingredients are incorporated. Place mixer on high and beat for 1 minute.

In another bowl, add flour, cinnamon, nutmeg, cloves, and ginger. Lightly stir. Fold in strawberries until they're coated in flour.

Fold dry ingredients into wet. Gently fold until all the flour has disappeared.

Pour batter into a greased and floured 9 x 5-inch loaf pan.

Bake in a 350°F preheated oven for 1 hour or until toothpick inserted into center comes out clean. Remove from oven. Let sit in pan for 10 minutes. Remove from pan and cool completely on wire rack.

Make glaze

Melt jam and butter. Add powdered sugar and lime juice. Whisk well. Add a few drops of milk if needed, and whisk until the glaze is thick but pourable.

Glaze bread when bread has completely cooled.

Chapter 4
SUMMER

Summer is the season of long, carefree days, blue skies, and a seemingly endless supply of sunshine. Kids delight to the sound of the ice cream truck rolling through the neighborhood, broadcasting a tune that seems to be written specifically for an ice cream truck. Pools, rivers, streams, and beaches offer a repose from summer's constant heat.

Southern kitchens ensure tea bags and lemons are on hand for the makings of sweet iced tea and lemonade to quench powerful thirsts brought on by long, hot days. A big glass of sweet iced tea serves double duty as thirst quencher and a gesture of Southern hospitality. Front porch sippin' material is part of our culture and an expectation of guests arriving at our decidedly Southern home.

As a child, my summers were split between time at home and at my grandparents' house. I grew up in an era when children weren't expected to stay underfoot but were required to spend most of the summer days outside. Times were much different. Activities viewed as neglectful parenting today were commonplace back then. Today, you must keep a watchful eye on children. Back then, we would check out after breakfast and might not return until later in the day. We'd explore the woods, hunt for tadpoles, build forts, play hide-n-seek, marvel at lightning bugs upon their arrival at dusk, and play various ball games in our street. If we got thirsty, we drank from the water hose. If we got hot, we rested in the shade. Visits to my grandparents' house meant blackberry picking, fishing, swimming, lots of church, hanging clothes on the clothesline to dry, pea picking and shelling, and swatting mosquitoes on the front porch after dark. So much has changed.

The activities that we considered fun might not seem like it next to today's electronic forms of entertainment, but I wouldn't trade those memories and experiences for anything. Not only have the forms of entertainment changed, but so have many of the marvels of nature that thrilled us. I don't know the last time I saw lightning bugs, tadpoles, or wild blackberry patches. Perhaps land development has something to do with that, but when I have the occasion to roam in the country from time to time, I still don't find any of them.

Speaking of another fixture of my childhood no longer present, I don't remember when I saw a bookmobile last. I've loved to read my entire life and always looked forward to the bookmobile coming into our neighborhood during the summer. It was an extension of the public library so you could check out books as long as you had a valid library card. There was something special about the bookmobile bringing books to the neighborhood instead of the neighborhood going to the library.

As much as the heat is hard for me to tolerate nowadays, I have to remind myself that I grew up in the Deep South without air conditioning. Honest to Pete, I don't know how on Earth we managed. But, managed we did. We were hot; all day long we were hot. PE was a requirement and we had it every day, regardless of the heat. I suppose we stayed a sweaty mess until mid-October when we got a little reprieve.

I long for the days when I looked forward to summer. We've lived in central Florida since 1985 and the summers are extended. And hot. And humid. And hot. And humid. And long. I don't appreciate summer like I did when I was a child. My current viewpoint of summer is that I must survive it instead of looking forward to the joy of the season. We travel to milder climates to get a break from the heat and humidity and that does improve my attitude, if only for a short while. I need to view the summer, once again, through the lens of a small child. One thing that may help is re-creating some of my favorite summer recipes from the past.

SUMMER RECIPES

Baked Sweet Potatoes with Chocolate Chips and Marshmallows
115

Barbeque Stuffed Sweet Potatoes
116

Microwave Sweet Potato Chips
120

Ham, Green Beans, and Sweet Potato Foil Packet
123

Ham, Sweet Potato, and Pineapple Foil Packet
124

Chipotle Brown Sugar Glazed Sweet Potatoes
125

Roasted Summer Berries with Sweet Potato Pone
127

Roasted Tomato and Basil Salad with Sweet Potato Cornbread Croutons
128

Roasted Sage Vegetable Salad with Sorghum Vinaigrette
131

Shari's Blueberry Thyme Butter
132

Skillet Sweet Potato and Blackberry Upside-Down Cake
135

Sweet Potato Ice Cream
138

Sweet Potato Oatmeal Scotchies
141

Sweet Potato Zucchini Muffins
142

Parmesan Roasted Sweet Potatoes with Comeback Sauce
145

BAKED SWEET POTATOES WITH CHOCOLATE CHIPS AND MARSHMALLOWS

Preheat oven to 400°F
Yield: 6 servings

If your only experience with the sweet potato/marshmallow combo is sweet potato casserole with marshmallow topping, I'm here to introduce a fun way to marry the two. Marshmallows are sugar and vanilla so that makes them a perfect flavor candidate for a marriage to sweet potatoes. S'mores taught us that chocolate and marshmallows belong together. Logically, it follows that if marshmallows and chocolate go together, and if marshmallows and sweet potatoes go together, then sweet potatoes, chocolate, and marshmallows are shoo-ins. Make these outdoors at a camp or tailgate site and use roasted jumbo marshmallows. Have the sweet potatoes baked and sprinkled with chocolate chips, then top with roasted marshmallows. Or, use the indoor method described below. I shared these with my friend Sheryl Francavilla thinking her children would enjoy them. Her son said he can't wait for this cookbook to come out so he can have more.

3 sweet potatoes, scrubbed
6 tablespoons milk chocolate chips, approximately
1½ cups miniature marshmallows, approximately

Bake the sweet potatoes at 400°F for 40 minutes or until they're soft. Remove from oven. As soon as you can handle them but before they cool completely, split in half, lengthwise. Sprinkle each half with approximately 1 tablespoon of milk chocolate chips. Lightly press the chips into the flesh to help them melt. Sprinkle marshmallows on the top of each half. Broil them for a couple of minutes or until they start to brown. Serve immediately.

BARBEQUE STUFFED SWEET POTATOES

Preheat oven to 400°F
Yield: 4 servings

Baked sweet potatoes are popular side dishes at Southern barbeque restaurants and smokehouses. With a little bit of leftover barbequed pork, beef, or chicken, a baked sweet potato is transformed into a meal. It's a great way to stretch leftovers. Don't ever throw away barbeque meat. South of the Mason-Dixon Line, it's considered a felony.

4 medium-sized sweet potatoes
olive oil
kosher salt
leftover shredded barbeque pork, beef, or chicken (approximately 12 ounces)
sour cream
chili powder
green onions, sliced
barbeque sauce

Wash and pat dry sweet potatoes. Rub skins with oil and sprinkle with kosher salt. Bake in a 400°F oven for 45 minutes or until soft.

When cool enough to handle, make a split in the sweet potatoes, but don't cut all the way through. Smoosh the ends toward the middle to make the sweet potato puff up.

Divide the barbeque meat between the sweet potatoes and place it in the pocket. Add a dollop of sour cream atop each potato. Sprinkle with chili powder. Garnish with green onions. Drizzle barbeque sauce over each potato.

Sweet Potatoes Are for Families with Young Children . . .

The kitchen is a learning laboratory for children. In addition to sparking creativity, they learn math by measuring, science by food chemistry, and reading from recipes. Plus, children are more inclined to eat a dish if they've helped in the preparation. With age-appropriate supervision, the kitchen is a safe place for children.

Jackson and Ella are my six-year-old twin grandchildren. They're also my only grand-children. They've enjoyed helping in the kitchen since they learned to stand. It's especially important to get them in the kitchen now that they're going through a picky-eater phase. My daughter, Amy, is a wonderful cook and makes a variety of nutritious meals for her family. Actually, Jackson and Ella aren't the only picky eaters in the family. Their dad, David, is also rather picky about what he eats.

Microwave sweet potato chips are a family-friendly dish that the whole family can enjoy making and eating. Kids need help slicing and possibly peeling sweet potatoes, depending on their age. The use of the microwave takes away the danger of burns from a conventional oven.

The sweetness of the sweet potato plus the salty sprinkle of kosher salt is a flavor combination that kids love. This dish is so quick and easy, it can be a side for a busy weeknight meal. The microwave doesn't heat up the kitchen like a conventional oven, which makes this a great summer dish.

Maybe Jackson and Ella will soon outgrow their picky-eater phase. Hopefully, they will maintain their interest in kitchen activities. Truth be told, they probably have a normal level of palate sophistication for six-year-olds. Their taste buds will continue to mature and help widen their list of acceptable foods. As for David, we've more than likely gotten all we're going to get in the way of adventurous eating.

MICROWAVE SWEET POTATO CHIPS

Yield: 4 servings

2 small to medium-sized sweet potatoes
olive oil
kosher salt

Cut a piece of parchment paper to fit a microwave-safe plate or the microwave turntable.

With a sharp knife, slice sweet potatoes no more than ⅛ of an inch thick. Place them in a large bowl. Drizzle with oil. Toss to coat well.

Place sweet potato pieces in a single layer on parchment paper. Sprinkle with kosher salt.

Microwave sweet potatoes on high for 3 minutes or until crisp. Keep an eye on them. Microwaves heat at different temperatures. Depending on the thickness of the potato slices, cooking times will vary.

When crisp, remove to another piece of parchment paper. Sprinkle with additional kosher salt, if desired.

HAM, GREEN BEANS, AND SWEET POTATO FOIL PACKET

Yield: 1 serving

For camping and grilling, foil packets are a fun and practical way to eat. You cook and eat in the same vessel, and when you're done, throw it away. Canned green beans may be substituted for fresh if that's more convenient. Take care when opening the packets after cooking, as they create lots of steam when cooking. For another foil packet cooking idea, see Ham, Sweet Potatoes, and Pineapple (recipe on page 124).

½ cup fresh greens beans, washed and trimmed
½ medium-sized sweet potato, peeled and diced into ½-inch cubes
½ small Yukon gold potato, peeled and diced into ½-inch cubes
1 tablespoon fresh thyme leaves
1 tablespoon sweet onion, finely minced
1 tablespoon unsalted butter, cubed
4–6 ounces fully cooked ham, cubed
salt and pepper, to taste

On a large sheet of heavy-duty aluminum foil, place green beans. Alongside the green beans, place the potatoes. Sprinkle thyme and onion atop the vegetables. Dot with butter.

Scatter the ham evenly across the top of the vegetables. Season with salt and pepper.

Fold the aluminum foil securely to contain the juices, but leave room for the packet to expand with steam. Place on a grill or over a campfire.

Cook for 25–30 minutes or until the vegetables are tender.

NOTE

For a spicy version, substitute fully cooked smoked sausage for the ham.

HAM, SWEET POTATO, AND PINEAPPLE FOIL PACKET

Yield: 1 serving

Sweet and salty is a winning flavor combination. Sweet potatoes, pineapple, and raisins create a taste inspired by sweet potato casserole. Ham cubes placed on top give the mixture a touch of salty ham goodness as the juices from the ham season as it cooks. Place the packet on the grill or on a grate over the campfire. Take care when opening the packet. Steam can burn your skin just like fire. For another foil packet idea, *see Ham, Green Beans, and Potatoes on page 123.*

½ medium-sized sweet potato, peeled and diced into ½-inch cubes
2 slices canned pineapple, cubed
½ ounce raisins
1 tablespoon pineapple juice
1 tablespoon brown sugar
1 tablespoon unsalted butter, cubed
4–6 ounces fully cooked ham, cut into 1-inch cubes
salt and pepper, to taste

On a large piece of heavy-duty aluminum foil, place sweet potatoes, pineapple, and raisins. Pour in pineapple juice. Sprinkle with brown sugar and butter cubes.

Spread ham cubes evenly over top. Season with salt and pepper.

Wrap foil securely but not tightly. Allow room for steam inside the packet. Cook on grill or over campfire for 25–30 minutes or until sweet potatoes are tender. Taste for seasoning and make adjustments.

CHIPOTLE BROWN SUGAR GLAZED SWEET POTATOES

Preheat oven to 400°F
Yield: 4 servings

The smoky sweet flavor of chipotle is a natural combination for the hearty flavor of a good, backyard-grilled steak. While a baked sweet potato is a wonderful side for a steak in and of itself, add the flavor of chipotle plus brown sugar for caramelization and you've got a blue ribbon in the making. Chipotle is smoked jalapeños in adobo sauce. The flavor is intense. My tolerance for heat is about one rung above wimpish, so I removed the seeds from the pepper to reduce the amount of heat. You decide how brave you want to be.

2 medium-sized whole sweet potatoes, washed and scrubbed
2 tablespoons brown sugar
2 tablespoons butter
1–2 chipotle peppers, seeds removed, finely minced
kosher salt for sprinkling

Peel sweet potatoes, if desired. (I desire to leave the peelings on.)

Cut the sweet potato in half. Cut each half into 4 wedges, lengthwise, and then cut the wedges in half, crosswise. You want 8 pieces from each half. Place in a large bowl.

Add brown sugar, butter, and minced chipotle peppers to a saucepan. Warm over medium heat until sugar has dissolved. Pour glaze over potatoes in the bowl. Stir to coat well.

Arrange the coated potato wedges in a single layer on a parchment paper–lined baking sheet.

Bake at 400°F for 30 minutes or until the potatoes are cooked through. Flip over, sprinkle with salt, and bake for an additional 10 minutes.

ROASTED SUMMER BERRIES WITH SWEET POTATO PONE

Preheat oven to 350°F
Yield: 8 servings

I grew up with cornbread pone that was simply unleavened cornmeal, water, and salt cooked in grease. The outside was crunchy and the inside a pudding-like consistency. I took inspiration for sweet potato pone from a recipe sent to me by my dear friend Shari Keen, who found it in a vintage Maryland cookbook. Roasting berries intensifies the flavor. Substitute any berry of your choosing. Adjust the amount of sugar according to the sweetness of the berries.

Berries:

4–6 cups blackberries
1 pint blueberries, approximately
½ cup brown sugar
1–2 cinnamon sticks
1 medium orange, sliced and seeds removed
1 lemon, sliced and seeds removed

Sweet potato pone:

¼ cup unsalted butter
¼ cup granulated sugar
¼ cup brown sugar
2 large eggs
1 medium-sized sweet potato, baked, cooled, and peeled
zest of 1 orange
1 teaspoon cinnamon
¼ teaspoon ginger
¼ teaspoon nutmeg
½ cup buttermilk

Make berries

Place all ingredients in a large baking dish. Roast for 1 hour. Before serving, remove citrus and cinnamon stick. Stir.

Make pone

Cream butter and both sugars. Add remaining ingredients and mix with electric mixer until the mixture is smooth. Pour into a 9-inch buttered cast-iron skillet. Bake at 350°F for 1 hour or until center is set.

To assemble

Pour berries in individual serving bowls. Place a scoop of sweet potato pone on top. Add a dollop of whipped cream.

ROASTED TOMATO AND BASIL SALAD WITH SWEET POTATO CORNBREAD CROUTONS

Preheat oven to 400°F
Yield: 4 side servings

My childhood friend frequently spoke of her mother's tomato salad which was a staple at their home during the summer. Her mother diced fresh tomatoes, seasoned with salt and pepper, and tossed with mayonnaise and crumbled saltine crackers. I took inspiration from my friend's beloved childhood memory and came up with this version using roasted tomatoes and sweet potato cornbread croutons. Make the cornbread recipe on page 71 and save a little bit for croutons.

1 cup sweet potato cornbread croutons (see cornbread recipe page 71)
5 Roma tomatoes, trimmed and cut in half lengthwise
olive oil
salt and pepper
¼ cup fresh basil leaves, cut into thin strips
¼ sweet onion, cut into thin rings
¼ cup goat cheese crumbles

Cut cornbread into 1-inch cubes and place on a baking sheet covered in parchment paper. Place in a 400°F oven and bake until lightly toasted. Remove and set aside.

Place Roma tomato halves on a baking sheet covered with parchment paper. Drizzle with olive oil and season with salt and pepper. Roast at 400°F for 1 hour. Remove and let cool.

Place roasted tomatoes on a platter. Top with basil and sweet onions. Drizzle with additional olive oil, if needed.

Add croutons and sprinkle with goat cheese crumbles.

ROASTED SAGE VEGETABLE SALAD WITH SORGHUM VINAIGRETTE

Preheat oven to 350°F

Yield: 4 servings main course, 6–8 side

If you haven't figured it out yet, I haven't met a vegetable I don't like roasted. This recipe makes a wonderful vegetarian meal or side dish. It's packable and will be happy going along for your summer picnics.

My sweet friend, Jean Sherrill, gifted me a jar of sorghum syrup. She grew up with it and wanted me to try it. Cane syrup was the table syrup in our house so we never had sorghum. It adds just the right touch of sweetness and flavor to the vinaigrette.

Vegetables:

8 ounces mushrooms, sliced
1 medium sweet onion, sliced in ½-inch-thick half moons
1 sweet bell pepper, cut into strips (choose any color)
8 ounces carrots, cut into 1-inch dice
1 medium-sized sweet potato, cut in 1-inch dice
2 cups cherry tomatoes
3 tablespoons fresh sage, minced
olive oil
salt and pepper

Sorghum vinaigrette:

1 cup salad oil
⅓ cup apple cider vinegar
1 tablespoon sorghum syrup (substitute cane syrup or maple, if desired)
1 tablespoon fresh chives, minced
½ teaspoon kosher salt
½ teaspoon garlic powder

Roast vegetables

Place first seven ingredients in a large bowl. Drizzle with olive oil and season with salt and pepper. Toss together until all vegetables are well-coated. Add more olive oil as needed.

Divide the vegetables among two large parchment-covered sheet pans

Roast at 350°F until all vegetables are soft and brown to your degree of liking.

Drizzle with sorghum vinaigrette before serving. Serve warm or room temperature.

Make vinaigrette

Whisk all ingredients together.

SHARI'S BLUEBERRY THYME BUTTER

Yield: ½ cup compound butter

Shari Keen shared her blueberry thyme homemade preserves with me. As soon as she handed it to me, I knew exactly how I wanted to use them: bring summer to a baked potato with blueberry thyme butter. Her preserves are perfect with just the right amount of thyme to accent the blueberries. If you're not as fortunate as me and don't have a blueberry thyme preserve–making friend, buy the best quality you can find; preserves, not friends. True friends can't be bought.

2 tablespoons blueberry thyme preserves
½ stick unsalted butter, room temperature

I chose to swirl the preserves into the butter instead of whipping it all together because I wanted the blueberries to remain intact and to let some of the natural butter color show through instead of turning the whole thing purple.

Place the softened butter on a piece of wax paper. With a spoon, spread the butter to about ¼ inch thick. Dot with preserves. Drag a spoon across the butter to distribute the preserves.

Roll the butter in the wax paper and reshape into a log. Thoroughly chill for at least 2 hours before using.

To serve butter, cut into slices and slather on a piping baked sweet potato.

SKILLET SWEET POTATO AND BLACKBERRY UPSIDE-DOWN CAKE

Preheat oven to 350°F
Yield: 6–8 servings

Upside-down cakes are a favorite of mine. They're not a heap of trouble to assemble and are small enough that you aren't left with a big layer cake that languishes on your kitchen counter and calls your name every time you enter the room. The choice of toppings is only limited to your imagination. I coupled sweet potatoes with my favorite summer berry: blackberries.

1 medium to large sweet potato
½ cup unsalted butter
½ cup brown sugar, firmly packed
1 teaspoon ground cinnamon
½ teaspoon ground ginger
½ teaspoon ground nutmeg
1 cup whole blackberries
5 tablespoons unsalted butter, room temperature
¾ cup granulated sugar
½ cup buttermilk
2 large eggs
2 teaspoons vanilla extract
1½ cups self-rising flour

Wash sweet potato and wrap in foil. Bake at 400°F until soft but not mushy. Remove from oven and let cool. As soon as the potato is cool enough to handle, unwrap and peel. Cut the potato in 8 rounds of equal thickness. Remove a section from the center of each round using an apple corer. The sweet potato rounds should resemble the shape of canned pineapple slices. Set sweet potato rounds and centers aside.

Add next five ingredients to a 9- or 10-inch cast-iron skillet over medium heat. Stir until sugar is dissolved. Remove from heat.

As soon as the skillet is cool enough, arrange sweet potatoes and blackberries in the skillet.

In a large mixing bowl, cream 5 tablespoons of butter and granulated sugar at room temperature. Mix in buttermilk and eggs. Add vanilla. Stir in flour until well-combined.

Pour batter on top of sweet potatoes and blackberries in the skillet. Gently spread evenly. Bake in a 350°F preheated oven for 40 minutes or until toothpick inserted comes out clean. Remove from oven and let cool for 5 minutes.

Run a knife along edges to loosen cake. Carefully place a serving plate on top of the skillet. Flip the skillet and plate over.

Sweet Potatoes Are for Sweet Potato Skeptics

My husband, Sam, doesn't include sweet potato among his favorite foods. He never learned to love them; the overwhelming reason being that he doesn't think he likes them so he won't try them. He will eat a boatload of white potatoes any day of the week, though, so he sticks to whites and doesn't dare venture over to the sweet potato. I wouldn't classify him as a picky eater. If he likes to eat something, he likes it "real good." However, he's not the most adventurous of eaters and isn't keen on trying new things. Sometimes, he's not keen on trying old things that are new to him, either. But, like everyone else on the planet, he loves ice cream. I came up with a recipe for sweet potato ice cream with spiced pecans and marshmallows that even the sweet potato skeptic loves.

SWEET POTATO ICE CREAM

Preheat oven to 350°F
Yield: approximately 2½ quarts

The best of sweet potato pie and sweet potato casserole are found in this luscious frozen treat. Spiced pecans and marshmallows are added in for extra flavor to an already flavorful ice cream base. Allow yourself enough time for this recipe. The base must be well chilled before it goes in the ice cream freezer.

Spiced pecans:

½ cup granulated sugar
½ teaspoon cayenne pepper
¾ teaspoon kosher salt
3 tablespoons water
2 cups pecans, halved

Ice cream:

4 cups half-and-half
2 cups heavy whipping cream
1½ cups granulated sugar
½ cup brown sugar
2 tablespoons vanilla extract
1 medium-sized sweet potato (approximately 1½ cups), baked, cooled, and peeled
2 teaspoon ground cinnamon
½ teaspoon ground nutmeg
½ teaspoon ground ginger
2 cups miniature marshmallows
1 cup spiced pecans, roughly chopped

Make spiced pecans

Add all ingredients, except pecans, to a heavy saucepan. Bring to a boil and cook for 2 minutes, stirring constantly. Remove from heat, add pecans to pan, and stir to coat. Pour onto a baking sheet covered in parchment paper. Separate, as best you can, with two forks sprayed with a nonstick cooking spray. Bake for 12 minutes or until pecans start to brown. Remove from oven and set aside.

Make ice cream

Add half-and-half, whipping cream, granulated sugar, and brown sugar to a large, heavy saucepan over medium heat. Whisk constantly until sugar is dissolved. Remove from heat. Add vanilla extract. In a medium bowl, add sweet potato, cinnamon, nutmeg, and ginger. Mash sweet potato and stir well.

Whisk sweet potato mixture into saucepan containing dairy and sugar. Strain mixture through a mesh sieve into a large bowl. Store covered in refrigerator overnight or at least 4 hours. Pour mixture into ice cream freezer and follow manufacturer's directions. Once mixture begins to freeze but is still soft, remove from ice cream freezer. In a freezer-safe container, alternate layers of the soft ice cream mixture with marshmallows and pecans. Cover and store in freezer. Serve after it has hardened. Garnish with additional spiced pecans.

SWEET POTATO OATMEAL SCOTCHIES

Preheat oven to 350°F
Yield: 1 (9 x 13-inch) pan

Butterscotch—you either love it or hate it. I fall into the love camp. Of course, there's no reason for me not to love it: it contains sugar. Brownies, blondies (brownies, chocolate-less first cousins), and bar cookies are less time-intensive than cookies. Once the batter is mixed, it goes into a pan to bake, negating the laborious task of dropping spoonfuls of dough into several batches. Cook up a batch of these for your next beach outing. Sweet potatoes, oatmeal, and coconut make butterscotch better than you can imagine.

2½ cups all-purpose flour
1 cup shredded coconut, sweetened
1 cup quick cooking rolled oats
2 teaspoons ground cinnamon
1 teaspoon baking powder
½ teaspoon ground ginger
½ teaspoon ground nutmeg
½ teaspoon kosher salt, plus more for sprinkling on top
1 cup unsalted butter, room temperature
1½ cups brown sugar, firmly packed
1 medium-sized sweet potato, baked and peeled
2 eggs
1 tablespoon vanilla extract
2 cups (12 ounces) butterscotch chips, divided

Grease a 9 x 13-inch pan and line with parchment paper. Greasing the pan helps to keep the parchment paper in place.

Measure dry ingredients (first eight ingredients) into a large bowl and set aside.

Cream butter and brown sugar with electric mixer. Mix in sweet potato, eggs, and vanilla extract. With mixer going, slowly add in dry ingredients just until incorporated. Don't overmix. Stir in about 1¼ cups butterscotch chips. Pour batter into pan and spread evenly.

Sprinkle remaining butterscotch chips on the top of the batter and gently press. Sprinkle with kosher salt.

Bake in a 350°F preheated oven for 40 minutes or until toothpick inserted comes out clean.

Remove from pan and cool on rack.

SWEET POTATO ZUCCHINI MUFFINS

Preheat oven to 350°F
Yield: approximately 18 muffins

Zucchini grows very well in our area—so well that backyard gardeners, like me, always scramble to find uses for the end of zucchini season. Just when you think you're about "zucchini-ed out" and looking for an end to the prolific crop, it seems to catch a second wind and sends out new blooms, which means more zucchini. Cook up big batches of these muffins and freeze some for later. They're wonderful to keep on hand for unexpected visitors. I took these along to a meeting I had with Jenn Blessing, director of Children's Ministries at our church. Jenn shared them with her family and I'm proud to report they were given the seal of approval from the Blessing family. Blessings come in many different forms.

1 cup all-purpose flour
1 cup whole wheat flour
2 teaspoons baking powder
2 teaspoons ground cinnamon
¼ teaspoon kosher salt
1 medium-sized sweet potato, peeled and grated (about 1½ cups)
1 large zucchini, grated (about 1½ cups)
¾ cup granulated sugar
¾ cup brown sugar
¾ cup vegetable oil
3 large eggs
2 teaspoons vanilla extract

Add both flours, baking powder, cinnamon, and salt to a bowl. Whisk together. Stir grated sweet potato and zucchini into flour mixture until well coated. Set aside.

With an electric mixer, beat both sugars and oil until smooth. Add in eggs, one at a time, beating after each addition. Add vanilla extract.

Stir together dry and wet ingredients only until all the flour disappears.

Line a muffin tin with paper liners or grease and flour each muffin cup. Divide the batter among the muffin cups. Bake in a 350°F preheated oven for 35 to 40 minutes or until inserted toothpick comes out clean.

PARMESAN ROASTED SWEET POTATOES WITH COMEBACK SAUCE

Preheat oven to 400°F
Yield: 4 servings potatoes | 1 pint comeback sauce

These roasted sweet potato wedges are fine just on their own, but the addition of comeback sauce as a dipping sauce adds another tasty dimension. If you confess to anyone from Mississippi that you've never heard of comeback sauce, they're likely to look at you like you've got two heads. This sauce was created by a restaurant owner in Jackson, Mississippi, and is certainly a recipe you'll want to keep at your fingertips. In addition to a dipping sauce for vegetables, it's equally delicious with seafood and chicken. It makes a wonderful sandwich spread and salad dressing, too. It goes with EVERYTHING—except Cheerios. Make comeback sauce the day before. It's better the next day. Store the extra in your refrigerator for as long as you'd keep condiments like ketchup and mayonnaise.

Roasted sweet potatoes:

2 medium-sized sweet potatoes, unpeeled and cut in eighths
½ cup olive oil
¼ cup grated Parmesan cheese
1 teaspoon seasoned salt
1 teaspoon dry Italian seasoning
½ teaspoon garlic powder

Comeback sauce:

1 cup Duke's mayonnaise
¼ cup ketchup
¼ cup chili sauce (*do not* substitute Thai chili sauce)
1 heaping teaspoon Dijon mustard
1 teaspoon onion powder
½ teaspoon garlic powder
2 teaspoons Worcestershire sauce
1 teaspoon ground black pepper
¼ teaspoon Tabasco sauce
¼ cup light olive oil
juice of 1 lemon

Roast sweet potatoes

Put sweet potato wedges in a gallon storage bag. Whisk together remaining ingredients and add to bag with sweet potatoes. Coat the sweet potatoes well. Place sweet potatoes, skin-side up, on a large baking sheet lined with parchment paper. Roast in a 400°F preheated oven for 45 minutes or until outsides are browned and crispy and insides are soft. Serve with comeback sauce.

Make comeback sauce

Mix all ingredients well and store in refrigerator overnight. It needs to sit to let the flavors become "acquainted." They shouldn't rush into marriage.

Sweet Potato Cornbread, page 71.

RESOURCES

Bell, Jason
Tater Man
tatermaninc.com

California Sweetpotatoes
casweetpotatoes.com
P.O. Box 366
Livingston, CA 95334
info@casweetpotatoes.com

Carter and Sons Farms
Shannon Wilson, Manager
281 Hickory Grove Road
Lake Park, GA 31636
carterandsonsproduce@yahoo.com
(229) 539-6931

Davenport, Peggy
Davenport's Daily Delights
(813) 810-8513
DavenportsDailyDelights@gmail.com
Facebook: Davenport's Daily Delights

International Potato Center
cip@cgiar.org
Avenida La Molina 1895, La Molina
Apartado Postal 1558
Lima, Peru

Louisiana Sweet Potato Commission
Louisiana Department of Agriculture and Forestry
sweetpotato.org
5825 Florida Blvd.
Baton Rouge, LA 70806
(225) 922-1277

Mississippi Sweet Potato Council
mssweetpotato.org
P.O. Box 100
Vardaman, MS 38878

North Carolina Sweet Potato Commission
Kelly McIver, executive director
kelly@ncsweetpotatoes.com
ncsweetpotatoes.com
700 E Parrish Drive, Suite C
Benson, NC 27504
(919) 894-1067

The United States Sweet Potato Council/American Sweet Potato Marketing Institute
sweetpotatousa.org
700 E. Parrish Drive, Suite C
Benson, NC 27504
(919) 894-1067

ACKNOWLEDGMENTS

Marcia, Amy, David, Jackson, Ella, Tyler, and Jaclyn: thank you for playing along with me and supporting this project and giving me a chance to show you off.

Jason Bell: you arranged sweet potato farm tours, gifted sweet potatoes, and shared industry information. Your help is invaluable.

Kathy Anderson and Peggy Davenport: thank you for allowing me to feature you and your point of view.

Shari Keen: gifts of blueberry thyme preserves and sweet potatoes are sweet gifts from an even sweeter friend.

Melonie Hall and Sheryl Francavilla: you always said yes when I asked you to test my recipes.

Becky DeShazo-Westly: you help me stay strong and healthy. Buckhorn Springs Golf and Country Club: for the many offerings of sweet potato dishes you graciously accepted.

St. Andrew's UMC, Brandon, Florida: to my wonderful church family.

Nicole Frail: editor extraordinaire.

Friends: you're always there when I need you.

I thank you all from the bottom of my sweet potato heart!

BIBLIOGRAPHY

"Commodity Highlight: Sweet Potatoes," Johnson, Wilson, Worosz, Fields, Bond, for United States Department of Agriculture, May 1, 2015.

"Health Benefits: Sweet Potatoes Are a SUPER FOOD," avthomasproduce.com, February 20, 2016.

"The Real Thanksgiving Foods," Oxendine, Jaime, PowWows.com, November 20, 2011.

"Sweetpotato Facts and Figures," International Potato Center, February 15, 2016.

"What's New and Beneficial About Sweet Potatoes," The World's Healthiest Foods, whfoods.com, February 21, 2016.

INDEX

A
Adobo sauce
Sweet Potato Chipotle Hummus, 23
Apple and Sweet Potato Braids, 78–79
Apple butter, 28–29
Apple Butter Twice-Baked Sweet Potatoes, 30–31
Apple cider
Sweet Potato Apple Butter, 28–29
Apple Cider Braised Boston Butt with Sweet Potato Mash, 8–9
Apple Cider Brined Chicken and Sweet Potato Skillet, 21–22
Apple cider vinegar
Pulled Pork Tacos with Spicy Sweet Potato Slaw, 88–89
Apples
Apple and Sweet Potato Braids, 78–79
Apple Sweet Potato Fried Pies, 26–27
Key Lime Sweet Potato Bisque with Key Lime Cream, 57
Sweet Potato Apple Butter, 28–29
Apple Sweet Potato Fried Pies, 26–27
Asparagus
Roasted Sweet Potato, Asparagus, and Sweet Pea Pasta Salad, 106–107
Asparagus, Sweet Potato, and Leek Pie, 101

B
Bacon
Sweet Potato and Bacon Hash with Baked Eggs, 81
Sweet Potato Cornbread, 71
Bacon grease
Citrus Garlic Cornish Game Hens with Sweet Potato Cornbread Dressing, 69–70
Baked Sweet Potatoes with Chocolate Chips and Marshmallows, 114–115
Baked Sweet Potatoes with Rum Raisin Sauce, 82–83
Balsamic Glazed Sweet Potatoes and Leeks, 44–45
Banana chips
Maple Sweet Potato Granola Bars, 16–17

Bananas
Banana Sweet Potato Breakfast Bread, 46–47
Banana Sweet Potato Breakfast Bread, 46–47
Barbeque sauce
Barbeque Stuffed Sweet Potatoes, 116–117
Barbeque seasoning
Apple Cider Braised Boston Butt with Sweet Potato Mash, 8–9
Barbeque Stuffed Sweet Potatoes, 116–117
Basil
Roasted Tomato and Basil Salad with Sweet Potato Cornbread Croutons, 128–129
Bay leaf
Apple Cider Brined Chicken and Sweet Potato Skillet, 21–22
Beef
barbeque
Barbeque Stuffed Sweet Potatoes, 116–117
ground
Ground Beef, Sweet Potato, and Collard Skillet Dinner, 12–13
Belle's Sweet Potato Chewies, 85
Bell pepper
Caribbean Jerk Quinoa and Sweet Potato, 51
Roasted Sage Vegetable Salad with Sorghum Vinaigrette, 130–131
Roasted Sweet Potato, Asparagus, and Sweet Pea Pasta Salad, 106–107
Biscuits, refrigerator
Apple Sweet Potato Fried Pies, 26–27
Blackberries
Roasted Summer Berries with Sweet Potato Pone, 126–127
Skillet Sweet Potato and Blackberry Upside-Down Cake, 134–135
Blueberries
Roasted Summer Berries with Sweet Potato Pone, 126–127
Shari's Blueberry Thyme Butter, 132–133
Boston butt
Apple Cider Braised Boston Butt with Sweet Potato Mash, 8–9
Bourbon
Sweet Potato Pie with Gingersnap Cookie Crust and Bourbon Whipped Cream, 36–37
Bread
Rosemary Sweet Potato Flatbread, 92
Strawberry Sweet Potato Bread with Glaze, 109
Sweet Potato Cornbread, 71
Brine, 22
Brussels sprouts
Supper of Chicken and Vegetables, 42–43
Butter, Shari's Blueberry Thyme, 132–133
Buttermilk
Overnight Sweet Potato Belgian Waffles, 102–103
Roasted Summer Berries with Sweet Potato Pone, 126–127
Skillet Sweet Potato and Blackberry Upside-Down Cake, 134–135
Sweet Potato Cake Doughnuts with Vanilla Buttermilk Glaze, 64–65
Sweet Potato Cake with Coconut Custard Filling and Buttermilk Cinnamon Glaze, 67–68
Sweet Potato Cornbread, 71
Sweet Potato Skillet Cake with Broiled Coconut and Pecan Icing, 99–100

Butternut squash
Caribbean Jerk Quinoa and Sweet Potato, 51
Butterscotch
Sweet Potato Ice Cream, 140–141
C
Cabbage
Chicken, Potato, and Cabbage Bake, 52–53
Pulled Pork Tacos with Spicy Sweet Potato Slaw, 88–89
Cake
Skillet Sweet Potato and Blackberry Upside-Down Cake, 134–135
Strawberry Sweet Potato Bread with Glaze, 109
Sweet Potato Cake with Coconut Custard Filling and Buttermilk Cinnamon Glaze, 67–68
Sweet Potato Pound Cake with Meyer Lemon Glaze, 72–73
Sweet Potato Skillet Cake with Broiled Coconut and Pecan Icing, 99–100
Caribbean Jerk Quinoa and Sweet Potato, 51
Carrots
Apple Cider Braised Boston Butt with Sweet Potato Mash, 8–9
Key Lime Sweet Potato Bisque with Key Lime Cream, 57
Lentil, Sweet Potato, and Chipotle Pepper Chili, 58–59
Roasted Sage Vegetable Salad with Sorghum Vinaigrette, 130–131
Split Pea, Ham, and Sweet Potato Soup, 61
Supper of Chicken and Vegetables, 42–43
Cast iron skillet, 25
Cayenne
Apple Cider Braised Boston Butt with Sweet Potato Mash, 8–9
Key Lime Sweet Potato Bisque with Key Lime Cream, 57
Sweet Potato Ice Cream, 138–139
Cheddar cheese
Sweet Potato Cornbread, 71
Cheese. *See also* Cream cheese
cheddar
Sweet Potato Cornbread, 71
goat
Roasted Sweet Potato, Asparagus, and Sweet Pea Pasta Salad, 106–107
Roasted Tomato and Basil Salad with Sweet Potato Cornbread Croutons, 128–129
Gruyère, 101
Parmesan
Parmesan Roasted Sweet Potatoes with Comeback Sauce, 144–145
Chicken
barbeque
Barbeque Stuffed Sweet Potatoes, 116–117
Citrus Garlic Cornish Game Hens with Sweet Potato Cornbread Dressing, 69–70
Chicken, Potato, and Cabbage Bake, 52–53
Chicken stock
Citrus Garlic Cornish Game Hens with Sweet Potato Cornbread Dressing, 69–70
Ground Beef, Sweet Potato, and Collard Skillet Dinner, 12–13
Key Lime Sweet Potato Bisque with Key Lime Cream, 57
Lentil, Sweet Potato, and Chipotle Pepper Chili, 58–59

Sweet Potato and Pear Soup, 62–63
Chicken thighs
Apple Cider Brined Chicken and Sweet Potato Skillet, 21–22
Chicken, Potato, and Cabbage Bake, 52–53
Supper of Chicken and Vegetables, 42–43
Chickpeas
Sweet Potato Chipotle Hummus, 23
Chili pepper
Sweet Potato Chipotle Hummus, 23
Chili powder
Barbeque Stuffed Sweet Potatoes, 116–117
Lentil, Sweet Potato, and Chipotle Pepper Chili, 58–59
Chili sauce
Parmesan Roasted Sweet Potatoes with Comeback Sauce, 144–145
Chilled Strawberry Sweet Potato Soup, 55–56
Chipotle
Chipotle Brown Sugar Glazed Sweet Potatoes, 125
Lentil, Sweet Potato, and Chipotle Pepper Chili, 58–59
Sweet Potato Chipotle Hummus, 23
Chipotle Brown Sugar Glazed Sweet Potatoes, 125
Chips
Microwave Sweet Potato Chips, 120–121
Chives
Roasted Sage Vegetable Salad with Sorghum Vinaigrette, 130–131
Chocolate chips
Baked Sweet Potatoes with Chocolate Chips and Marshmallows, 114–115
Sweet Potato Chocolate Chip Cookies, 95
Christmas, 39–40
Cinnamon
Apple and Sweet Potato Braids, 78–79
Apple Butter Twice-Baked Sweet Potatoes, 30–31
Apple Sweet Potato Fried Pies, 26–27
Banana Sweet Potato Breakfast Bread, 46–47
Cranberry Glazed Sweet Potatoes, 5
Maple Sweet Potato Granola Bars, 16–17
Oatmeal Sweet Potato Cookies, 87
Overnight Sweet Potato Belgian Waffles, 102–103
Pecan and Sweet Potato Pie, 34–35
Roasted Summer Berries with Sweet Potato Pone, 126–127
Skillet Sweet Potato and Blackberry Upside-Down Cake, 134–135
Strawberry Sweet Potato Bread with Glaze, 109
Sweet Potato and Pear Soup, 62–63
Sweet Potato Apple Butter, 28–29
Sweet Potato Cake Doughnuts with Vanilla Buttermilk Glaze, 64–65
Sweet Potato Cake with Coconut Custard Filling and Buttermilk Cinnamon Glaze, 67–68
Sweet Potato Casserole with Pecan Oatmeal Crumble Topping, 6–7
Sweet Potato Chocolate Chip Cookies, 95
Sweet Potato Coconut Fritters, 96–97
Sweet Potato Ice Cream, 138–139, 140–141
Sweet Potato Muffins with Cranberry Pear Filling, 32–33

Sweet Potato Pear Cranberry Scones with Maple Ginger Glaze, 18–19
Sweet Potato Pie with Gingersnap Cookie Crust and Bourbon Whipped Cream, 36–37
Sweet Potato Pie with Vanilla Meringue, 15
Sweet Potato Pound Cake with Meyer Lemon Glaze, 72–73
Sweet Potato Skillet Cake with Broiled Coconut and Pecan Icing, 99–100
Sweet Potato Zucchini Muffins, 142–143
Citrus Garlic Cornish Game Hens with Sweet Potato Cornbread Dressing, 69–70
Cloves
Strawberry Sweet Potato Bread with Glaze, 109
Sweet Potato Pie with Gingersnap Cookie Crust and Bourbon Whipped Cream, 36–37
Sweet Potato Pie with Vanilla Meringue, 15
Coconut
Banana Sweet Potato Breakfast Bread, 46–47
Maple Sweet Potato Granola Bars, 16–17
Sweet Potato Cake Doughnuts with Vanilla Buttermilk Glaze, 64–65
Sweet Potato Cake with Coconut Custard Filling and Buttermilk Cinnamon Glaze, 67–68
Sweet Potato Coconut Fritters, 96–97
Sweet Potato Ice Cream, 140–141
Sweet Potato Skillet Cake with Broiled Coconut and Pecan Icing, 99–100
Coconut oil
Ground Beef, Sweet Potato, and Collard Skillet Dinner, 12–13
Collard greens
Ground Beef, Sweet Potato, and Collard Skillet Dinner, 12–13
Cookies
Oatmeal Sweet Potato Cookies, 87
Sweet Potato Chocolate Chip Cookies, 95
Sweet Potato Ice Cream, 140–141
Cornbread, 71
Cornish game hen
Citrus Garlic Cornish Game Hens with Sweet Potato Cornbread Dressing, 69–70
Cranberries
Cranberry Glazed Sweet Potatoes, 5
Maple Sweet Potato Granola Bars, 16–17
Sweet Potato Muffins with Cranberry Pear Filling, 32–33
Sweet Potato Pear Cranberry Scones with Maple Ginger Glaze, 18–19
Cranberry Glazed Sweet Potatoes, 5
Cream cheese
Apple and Sweet Potato Braids, 78–79
Sweet Potato Casserole with Pecan Oatmeal Crumble Topping, 6–7
Sweet Potato Pound Cake with Meyer Lemon Glaze, 72–73
Croutons
Roasted Tomato and Basil Salad with Sweet Potato Cornbread Croutons, 128–129

D
Dog treats, 85

E
Easter, 75
Eggs

Sweet Potato and Bacon Hash with Baked Eggs, 81

F
Fall, 1–37
Football, 1–2

G
Garlic
Apple Cider Braised Boston Butt with Sweet Potato Mash, 8–9
Apple Cider Brined Chicken and Sweet Potato Skillet, 21–22
Caribbean Jerk Quinoa and Sweet Potato, 51
Citrus Garlic Cornish Game Hens with Sweet Potato Cornbread Dressing, 69–70
Ground Beef, Sweet Potato, and Collard Skillet Dinner, 12–13
Key Lime Sweet Potato Bisque with Key Lime Cream, 57
Lentil, Sweet Potato, and Chipotle Pepper Chili, 58–59
Split Pea, Ham, and Sweet Potato Soup, 61
Sweet Potato Chipotle Hummus, 23
Ginger, 14
Apple Sweet Potato Fried Pies, 26–27
Banana Sweet Potato Breakfast Bread, 46–47
Cranberry Glazed Sweet Potatoes, 5
Pecan and Sweet Potato Pie, 34–35
Roasted Summer Berries with Sweet Potato Pone, 126–127
Skillet Sweet Potato and Blackberry Upside-Down Cake, 134–135
Strawberry Sweet Potato Bread with Glaze, 109
Sweet Potato Apple Butter, 28–29
Sweet Potato Cake Doughnuts with Vanilla Buttermilk Glaze, 64–65
Sweet Potato Coconut Fritters, 96–97
Sweet Potato Ice Cream, 138–139, 140–141
Sweet Potato Muffins with Cranberry Pear Filling, 32–33
Sweet Potato Pear Cranberry Scones with Maple Ginger Glaze, 18–19
Sweet Potato Pie with Gingersnap Cookie Crust and Bourbon Whipped Cream, 36–37
Sweet Potato Pie with Vanilla Meringue, 15
Sweet Potato Pound Cake with Meyer Lemon Glaze, 72–73
Sweet Potato Skillet Cake with Broiled Coconut and Pecan Icing, 99–100
Gingerbread cookies
Sweet Potato Pie with Gingersnap Cookie Crust and Bourbon Whipped Cream, 36–37
Goat cheese
Roasted Sweet Potato, Asparagus, and Sweet Pea Pasta Salad, 106–107
Roasted Tomato and Basil Salad with Sweet Potato Cornbread Croutons, 128–129
Gravy, 22
Greek yogurt
Chilled Strawberry Sweet Potato Soup, 55–56
Green beans
Ham, Green Beans, and Sweet Potato Foil Packet, 122–123
Ground Beef, Sweet Potato, and Collard Skillet Dinner, 12–13

Gruyère cheese
Asparagus, Sweet Potato, and Leek Pie, 101

H
Halloween, 2
Ham
Ham, Green Beans, and Sweet Potato Foil Packet, 122–123
Ham, Sweet Potato, and Pineapple Foil Packet, 124
Split Pea, Ham, and Sweet Potato Soup, 61
Ham, Green Beans, and Sweet Potato Foil Packet, 122–123
Ham, Sweet Potato, and Pineapple Foil Packet, 124
Honey
Chilled Strawberry Sweet Potato Soup, 55–56
Sweet Potato Casserole with Pecan Oatmeal Crumble Topping, 6–7
Hummus, 23

I
Ice cream
Sweet Potato Ice Cream, 138–139
Italian seasoning
Parmesan Roasted Sweet Potatoes with Comeback Sauce, 144–145

J
Jalapeños
Pulled Pork Tacos with Spicy Sweet Potato Slaw, 88–89

K
Ketchup
Parmesan Roasted Sweet Potatoes with Comeback Sauce, 144–145
Key Lime Sweet Potato Bisque with Key Lime Cream, 57

L
Leeks
Asparagus, Sweet Potato, and Leek Pie, 101
Balsamic Glazed Sweet Potatoes and Leeks, 44–45
Lemon
Roasted Summer Berries with Sweet Potato Pone, 126–127
Sweet Potato Apple Butter, 28–29
Lemon juice
Apple and Sweet Potato Braids, 78–79
Parmesan Roasted Sweet Potatoes with Comeback Sauce, 144–145
Strawberry Sweet Potato Bread with Glaze, 109
Sweet Potato Pound Cake with Meyer Lemon Glaze, 72–73
Lentil, Sweet Potato, and Chipotle Pepper Chili, 58–59
Lime juice
Strawberry Sweet Potato Bread with Glaze, 109

M
Maple Sweet Potato Granola Bars, 16–17
Maple syrup
Apple and Sweet Potato Braids, 78–79
Maple Sweet Potato Granola Bars, 16–17
Roasted Sage Vegetable Salad with Sorghum Vinaigrette, 130–131
Sweet Potato Pear Cranberry Scones with Maple Ginger Glaze, 18–19
Marshmallows
Baked Sweet Potatoes with Chocolate Chips and Marshmallows, 114–115

Sweet Potato Ice Cream, 138–139
Mayonnaise
Parmesan Roasted Sweet Potatoes with Comeback Sauce, 144–145
Pulled Pork Tacos with Spicy Sweet Potato Slaw, 88–89
Meringue
Sweet Potato Pie with Vanilla Meringue, 15
Meyer lemon juice
Apple and Sweet Potato Braids, 78–79
Sweet Potato Pound Cake with Meyer Lemon Glaze, 72–73
Microwave Sweet Potato Chips, 120–121
Mother's Day, 76
Muffins
Sweet Potato Muffins with Cranberry Pear Filling, 32–33
Sweet Potato Zucchini Muffins, 142–143
Mushrooms
Roasted Sage Vegetable Salad with Sorghum Vinaigrette, 130–131
Mustard
Apple Cider Braised Boston Butt with Sweet Potato Mash, 8–9
Parmesan Roasted Sweet Potatoes with Comeback Sauce, 144–145

N
Napa cabbage
Pulled Pork Tacos with Spicy Sweet Potato Slaw, 88–89
Nutmeg, 14
Apple Sweet Potato Fried Pies, 26–27
Banana Sweet Potato Breakfast Bread, 46–47
Oatmeal Sweet Potato Cookies, 87
Pecan and Sweet Potato Pie, 34–35
Roasted Summer Berries with Sweet Potato Pone, 126–127
Skillet Sweet Potato and Blackberry Upside-Down Cake, 134–135
Strawberry Sweet Potato Bread with Glaze, 109
Sweet Potato Apple Butter, 28–29
Sweet Potato Cake Doughnuts with Vanilla Buttermilk Glaze, 64–65
Sweet Potato Casserole with Pecan Oatmeal Crumble Topping, 6–7
Sweet Potato Coconut Fritters, 96–97
Sweet Potato Ice Cream, 138–139, 140–141
Sweet Potato Muffins with Cranberry Pear Filling, 32–33
Sweet Potato Pie with Gingersnap Cookie Crust and Bourbon Whipped Cream, 36–37
Sweet Potato Pie with Vanilla Meringue, 15
Sweet Potato Pound Cake with Meyer Lemon Glaze, 72–73

O
Oatmeal
Maple Sweet Potato Granola Bars, 16–17
Oatmeal Sweet Potato Cookies, 87
Sweet Potato Casserole with Pecan Oatmeal Crumble Topping, 6–7
Oatmeal Sweet Potato Cookies, 87
Oats
Sweet Potato Ice Cream, 140–141
Orange juice
Citrus Garlic Cornish Game Hens with Sweet Potato Cornbread Dressing, 69–70

Oranges
Chilled Strawberry Sweet Potato Soup, 55–56
Roasted Summer Berries with Sweet Potato Pone, 126–127
Overnight Sweet Potato Belgian Waffles, 102–103
P
Parmesan cheese
Parmesan Roasted Sweet Potatoes with Comeback Sauce, 144–145
Parmesan Roasted Sweet Potatoes with Comeback Sauce, 144–145
Parsley
Split Pea, Ham, and Sweet Potato Soup, 61
Pasta salad
Roasted Sweet Potato, Asparagus, and Sweet Pea Pasta Salad, 106–107
Pastry
Apple and Sweet Potato Braids, 78–79
Peanut butter
Maple Sweet Potato Granola Bars, 16–17
Peanuts
Banana Sweet Potato Breakfast Bread, 46–47
Pears
Sweet Potato and Pear Soup, 62–63
Sweet Potato Muffins with Cranberry Pear Filling, 32–33
Sweet Potato Pear Cranberry Scones with Maple Ginger Glaze, 18–19
Peas
Roasted Sweet Potato, Asparagus, and Sweet Pea Pasta Salad, 106–107
Split Pea, Ham, and Sweet Potato Soup, 61
Pecan and Sweet Potato Pie, 34–35
Pecans
Apple Sweet Potato Fried Pies, 26–27
Maple Sweet Potato Granola Bars, 16–17
Pecan and Sweet Potato Pie, 34–35
Sweet Potato Cake Doughnuts with Vanilla Buttermilk Glaze, 64–65
Sweet Potato Cake with Coconut Custard Filling and Buttermilk Cinnamon Glaze, 67–68
Sweet Potato Casserole with Pecan Oatmeal Crumble Topping, 6–7
Sweet Potato Ice Cream, 138–139
Peppercorns
Apple Cider Brined Chicken and Sweet Potato Skillet, 21–22
Pie
Apple Sweet Potato Fried Pies, 26–27
Asparagus, Sweet Potato, and Leek Pie, 101
Pecan and Sweet Potato Pie, 34–35
Sweet Potato Pie with Gingersnap Cookie Crust and Bourbon Whipped Cream, 36–37
Sweet Potato Pie with Vanilla Meringue, 15
Pineapple
Ham, Sweet Potato, and Pineapple Foil Packet, 124
Sweet Potato Cake with Coconut Custard Filling and Buttermilk Cinnamon Glaze, 67–68
Pineapple juice
Ham, Sweet Potato, and Pineapple Foil Packet, 124
Pork, pulled
Barbeque Stuffed Sweet Potatoes, 116–117

Pulled Pork Tacos with Spicy Sweet Potato Slaw, 88–89
Pork roast
Apple Cider Braised Boston Butt with Sweet Potato Mash, 8–9
Potatoes
Chicken, Potato, and Cabbage Bake, 52–53
Ham, Green Beans, and Sweet Potato Foil Packet, 122–123
Roasted Sweet and Yukon Gold Potatoes, 91
Supper of Chicken and Vegetables, 42–43
Puff pastry
Apple and Sweet Potato Braids, 78–79
Pulled Pork Tacos with Spicy Sweet Potato Slaw, 88–89

Q
Quinoa
Caribbean Jerk Quinoa and Sweet Potato, 51

R
Raisins
Apple Sweet Potato Fried Pies, 26–27
Baked Sweet Potatoes with Rum Raisin Sauce, 82–83
Banana Sweet Potato Breakfast Bread, 46–47
Ham, Sweet Potato, and Pineapple Foil Packet, 124
Oatmeal Sweet Potato Cookies, 87
Red pepper
Caribbean Jerk Quinoa and Sweet Potato, 51
Roasted Sweet Potato, Asparagus, and Sweet Pea Pasta Salad, 106–107
Roasted Sage Vegetable Salad with Sorghum Vinaigrette, 130–131
Roasted Summer Berries with Sweet Potato Pone, 126–127
Roasted Sweet and Yukon Gold Potatoes, 91
Roasted Sweet Potato, Asparagus, and Sweet Pea Pasta Salad, 106–107
Roasted Tomato and Basil Salad with Sweet Potato Cornbread Croutons, 128–129
Rosemary
Apple Cider Brined Chicken and Sweet Potato Skillet, 21–22
Roasted Sweet and Yukon Gold Potatoes, 91
Rosemary Sweet Potato Flatbread, 92
Sweet Potato and Bacon Hash with Baked Eggs, 81
Rosemary Sweet Potato Flatbread, 92
Rum
Baked Sweet Potatoes with Rum Raisin Sauce, 82–83

S
Sage
Apple Cider Brined Chicken and Sweet Potato Skillet, 21–22
Citrus Garlic Cornish Game Hens with Sweet Potato Cornbread Dressing, 69–70
Roasted Sage Vegetable Salad with Sorghum Vinaigrette, 130–131
Salad
Roasted Sweet Potato, Asparagus, and Sweet Pea Pasta Salad, 106–107
Roasted Tomato and Basil Salad with Sweet Potato Cornbread Croutons, 128–129

Shallots
  Apple Cider Brined Chicken and Sweet Potato Skillet, 21–22
Shari's Blueberry Thyme Butter, 132–133
Skillet, 25
  Apple Cider Brined Chicken and Sweet Potato Skillet, 21–22
  Ground Beef, Sweet Potato, and Collard Skillet Dinner, 12–13
Skillet Sweet Potato and Blackberry Upside Down Cake, 134–135
Slaw
  Pulled Pork Tacos with Spicy Sweet Potato Slaw, 88–89
Sorghum syrup
  Roasted Sage Vegetable Salad with Sorghum Vinaigrette, 130–131
Soup
  Chilled Strawberry Sweet Potato Soup, 55–56
  Split Pea, Ham, and Sweet Potato Soup, 61
  Sweet Potato and Pear Soup, 62–63
Sour cream
  Chilled Strawberry Sweet Potato Soup, 55–56
Soy sauce
  Citrus Garlic Cornish Game Hens with Sweet Potato Cornbread Dressing, 69–70
Split Pea, Ham, and Sweet Potato Soup, 61
Split peas
  Split Pea, Ham, and Sweet Potato Soup, 61
Spring, 75–109
Squash, butternut
  Caribbean Jerk Quinoa and Sweet Potato, 51
Strawberries
  Chilled Strawberry Sweet Potato Soup, 55
Strawberry jam
  Strawberry Sweet Potato Bread with Glaze, 109
Strawberry Sweet Potato Bread with Glaze, 109
Summer, 111–145
Supper of Chicken and Vegetables, 42–43
Sweet peas
  Roasted Sweet Potato, Asparagus, and Sweet Pea Pasta Salad, 106–107
Sweet Potato and Bacon Hash with Baked Eggs, 81
Sweet Potato and Pear Soup, 62–63
Sweet Potato Apple Butter, 28–29
Sweet Potato Cake Doughnuts with Vanilla Buttermilk Glaze, 64–65
Sweet Potato Cake with Coconut Custard Filling and Buttermilk Cinnamon Glaze, 67–68
Sweet Potato Casserole with Pecan Oatmeal Crumble Topping, 6–7
Sweet Potato Chipotle Hummus, 23
Sweet Potato Chocolate Chip Cookies, 95
Sweet Potato Coconut Fritters, 96–97
Sweet Potato Cornbread, 71
Sweet Potato Ice Cream, 138–139
Sweet Potato Muffins with Cranberry Pear Filling, 32–33
Sweet Potato Oatmeal Scotchies, 140–141
Sweet Potato Pear Cranberry Scones with Maple Ginger Glaze, 18–19
Sweet Potato Pie with Gingersnap Cookie Crust and Bourbon Whipped Cream, 36–37
Sweet Potato Pie with Vanilla Meringue, 15

Sweet Potato Pound Cake with Meyer Lemon Glaze, 72–73
Sweet Potato Skillet Cake with Broiled Coconut and Pecan Icing, 99–100
Sweet Potato Zucchini Muffins, 142–143

T
Tabasco sauce
  Parmesan Roasted Sweet Potatoes with Comeback Sauce, 144–145
Tacos
  Pulled Pork Tacos with Spicy Sweet Potato Slaw, 88–89
Tahini
  Sweet Potato Chipotle Hummus, 23
Thanksgiving, 2
Thyme
  Ham, Green Beans, and Sweet Potato Foil Packet, 122–123
  Shari's Blueberry Thyme Butter, 132–133
  Sweet Potato and Pear Soup, 62–63
Tomatoes
  Ground Beef, Sweet Potato, and Collard Skillet Dinner, 12–13
  Roasted Sage Vegetable Salad with Sorghum Vinaigrette, 130–131
  Roasted Tomato and Basil Salad with Sweet Potato Cornbread Croutons, 128–129
Tomato paste
  Lentil, Sweet Potato, and Chipotle Pepper Chili, 58–59

V
Vegetable broth
  Caribbean Jerk Quinoa and Sweet Potato, 51
Vegetarianism, 49

W
Waffles
  Overnight Sweet Potato Belgian Waffles, 102–103
Winter, 39–73
Worcestershire sauce
  Parmesan Roasted Sweet Potatoes with Comeback Sauce, 144–145

Y
Yellow pepper
  Roasted Sweet Potato, Asparagus, and Sweet Pea Pasta Salad, 106–107
Yogurt, Greek
  Chilled Strawberry Sweet Potato Soup, 55–56

Z
Zucchini
  Sweet Potato Zucchini Muffins, 142–143

CONVERSION CHARTS

METRIC AND IMPERIAL CONVERSIONS

(These conversions are rounded for convenience)

Ingredient	Cups/Tablespoons/ Teaspoons	Ounces	Grams/Milliliters
Butter	1 cup = 16 tablespoons = 2 sticks	8 ounces	230 grams
Cream cheese	1 tablespoon	0.5 ounce	14.5 grams
Cheese, shredded	1 cup	4 ounces	110 grams
Cornstarch	1 tablespoon	0.3 ounce	8 grams
Flour, all-purpose	1 cup/1 tablespoon	4.5 ounces/0.3 ounce	125 grams/8 grams
Flour, whole wheat	1 cup	4 ounces	120 grams
Fruit, dried	1 cup	4 ounces	120 grams
Fruits or veggies, chopped	1 cup	5 to 7 ounces	145 to 200 grams
Fruits or veggies, puréed	1 cup	8.5 ounces	245 grams
Honey, maple syrup, or corn syrup	1 tablespoon	.75 ounce	20 grams
Liquids: cream, milk, water, or juice	1 cup	8 fluid ounces	240 milliliters
Oats	1 cup	5.5 ounces	150 grams
Salt	1 teaspoon	0.2 ounce	6 grams
Spices: cinnamon, cloves, ginger, or nutmeg (ground)	1 teaspoon	0.2 ounce	5 milliliters
Sugar, brown, firmly packed	1 cup	7 ounces	200 grams
Sugar, white	1 cup/1 tablespoon	7 ounces/0.5 ounce	200 grams/12.5 grams
Vanilla extract	1 teaspoon	0.2 ounce	4 grams

OVEN TEMPERATURES

Fahrenheit	Celsius	Gas Mark
225°	110°	¼
250°	120°	½
275°	140°	1
300°	150°	2
325°	160°	3
350°	180°	4
375°	190°	5
400°	200°	6
425°	220°	7
450°	230°	8